# Gateway to Armenia

# About the Author

Serge Momjian was born in Beirut in 1946. He moved to London in the 1970s and studied journalism then took a degree course in creative writing.

He has worked as a reporter, covering arts and culture for major publications, including Beirut's *Daily Star* (the Middle East's leading English-language newspaper) and London's *Events* magazine. His feature articles have been translated and published in the Armenian press. By the time he reached his forties, he was devoting his time to writing novels. His works, all published in the United Kingdom, include *Conflicting Motives*, *The Invisible Line*, *The Singer of the Opera*, *Memories of the Past*, and *Komitas, The Artist and The Martyr*. The latter, in which he included dialogue for the first time, was written in commemoration of the centenary of the Armenian Genocide.

In recognition of his biographical work, he was awarded the William Saroyan medal in 2015 by the Ministry of Diaspora of the Republic of Armenia (RA). During his literary career his innovative writings have brought him praise and a good reputation.

# Gateway to Armenia

*One diasporan's journey
into the past and present*

**Serge Momjian**

**HEDDON PUBLISHING**

**United Kingdom**

First published in Great Britain 2018 by Heddon Publishing

www.heddonpublishing.com

Copyright © Serge Momjian 2018

A catalogue record for this book is available from the
British Library

ISBN 978-1-9995963-0-9

Cover Design: Serge Momjian and Catherine Clarke

Cover images from Armenian Travel Bureaus

**To the divine inspiration that helped me accomplish greater things in writing.**

# Acknowledgements

I would like to express my gratitude to the editor who provided exceptionally helpful feedback during the production process.

# Cover images

**From left to right:**

The Pegan Garni temple built by King Trdat in the first century AD.

The Amberd Fortress constructed in the seventh century by Armenian Prince Kamsarakan.

The Elite Plaza tower in Yerevan. Established in 2012, the business centre is home to many international companies and agencies.

# A note from the author

Western Armenians in the diaspora have successfully integrated into their respective host countries. There are those who have struggled to sustain their ethnic identity and traditions, and there are Armenians who have assimilated and surrendered their ethnicity as a result of changing their names or not speaking Armenian. For the latter, it is not surprising that they have very little, if no, knowledge of Armenian history, culture and literature. The fact that their ancestors were Armenian, and suffered and sacrificed so much, has no significance for them. They prefer to move on with their lives and use the national language of their home countries rather than their mother tongue. Haig Bedrossian, the American-Armenian protagonist in the novel, is no exception. However, being not fully assimilated into the immigrant country, he begins to reconsider his ethnic self-identity.

# Introduction

Since Armenia's independence in 1991, Armenians from the large overseas diaspora have been visiting their free homeland, which is no more than a dream and a forgotten Soviet province in the past. However, Armenia today remains largely unknown for foreign tourists as it has not yet realized its full tourism potential.

For the majority of descendants of Western diasporan Armenians, their "ancestral homeland" or the "historical homeland" constitutes the eastern parts of today's Turkey, which their forefathers had left before, during and after the genocide. These ethnic Armenians who came to discover or re-discover the present-day Armenia before the revolution in 2018 have experienced, along with locals, the bitter contrast between the "Armenian dream" of decent living, social justice, a promising future and success, against the grim realities of poverty, rampant corruption, unemployment and high-volume emigration.

Armenia, a tiny and landlocked country where Soviet legacy is still present, has been developing at a very slow pace of structural reform. However, there is an audience of young, emerging leaders who would like to take the country forward within the next few decades. Skilled diasporan Armenians are given the opportunity to apply the knowledge and experience they have gained in their host countries, while organizations such as Birthright Armenia and the Armenian Volunteer Corps (AVC) encourage diasporan youth to be part of Armenia's daily life and contribute to its development through volunteer experiences.

At the end of each year, during the Armenian Telethon, funds from the rich Armenian diaspora are raised in donations and pledges for many projects in Armenia and Nagorno-Karabakh. Proceeds from the Armenia Fund, a non-governmental and non-political organization, have gone to large-scale humanitarian and infrastructure development − building roads, schools, hospitals and polyclinics in Artsakh, and providing medical equipment.

Every summer, the country also hosts various festivals and international music competitions, which attract some worldwide attention.

Nevertheless, the majority of the diasporan Armenians find it hard to integrate into Armenia's society, due to conflicting patterns of life. Moreover, what they see is an uncertain future in a volatile region and a lack of opportunities for themselves. Others are optimistic, saying that twenty-five years for a new state is not long; it would take some time to clean the whole system of old habits, outmoded attitudes and beliefs. Some from this group have already settled in the homeland and begun a new life in the hope of a better future.

But all of them - diasporan Armenians and foreigners alike - admit that Armenia is beautiful, with a rich cultural heritage and a recorded history of almost 4000 years; a country where historic sites, mystical monasteries and old legends together with the new modern capital city in transition typify the harmonious fusion of past and present.

# Chapter 1

I did not really know what it meant to be an Armenian today, in a multi-ethnic and multicultural American "melting pot" society. Born in Boston, the only son of Armenian immigrant parents who arrived in the 1970s, I, Haig Bedrossian, had lived outside my ethnic community virtually all my life. My education was American; my classmates and friends, who came from different ethnic backgrounds, were American citizens; the locals, with whom I interacted daily in our neighbourhood, were a mix of various ethnic groups – Puerto Rican and Dominican Americans, Salvadorans, Guatemalans, some Mexicans, and others. Our common language was American English and we possessed an allegiance to our country, thus embracing its democratic and liberal values.

I hardly ever heard about Armenia and only knew that Christianity and Noah's Ark had something to do with it. The picture of Mount Ararat which hung on the wall in our house was a reminder of this distant country.

As a senior journalist at the *Boston Daily*, a local English-language newspaper, I had a gruelling schedule, working under pressure to tight deadlines. I was so absorbed in office work that I didn't know how the months and years flew by until a major, unique event occurred, which would shape the course of my future life. On 24 April 2015, hundreds of thousands of Armenians worldwide commemorated the centenary of the Armenian Genocide. Turkey was accused of the deaths of 1.5 million innocent people.

It just clicked with me that something which had been brushed away for ages was now jolted out of its dormancy like a volcanic eruption - my Armenian-ness.

I watched quietly the huge demonstrations on the TV as tens of thousands of determined Armenians in the big cities marched solemnly, carrying wide banners reading: 'Turkey Guilty of Genocide' and 'Turkey Will Pay'.

I thought maybe a terrible injustice had been committed against the Armenians in the past.

Candles were lit in the Armenian Trinity Church in Boston, in remembrance of all those who perished. But Turkey adamantly denied the claim that its predecessors had perpetrated a genocide. At this point, I did not know the truth about this great calamity, nor did I hear anything about it. I said to myself that if it really happened, it was a crime against humanity and an immense tragedy.

The following day, I felt a sudden twinge of guilt for having ignored my ethnic identity. Like an ethnocentric Armenian, my father had desperately tried to implant Armenian-ness in me from a young age but I did not care at the time. He once shouted at me as I enthusiastically talked to him about American values, 'Stop it, you little stubborn kid, I want you to feel Armenian, your opinions will never matter to me. Go on, get lost!' His words had sounded like an order and I quickly ran back to my room. I was in fact a stubborn child, which perhaps helped me to be successful later in my career.

The recall of his remark came now as a moral reawakening to my busy life. But I was wondering how I would be able to feel and think Armenian and if that new feeling in me would somehow match my real-life identities. The perceptual and functional understanding of Armenian identity in the 21$^{st}$ century seemed a complex issue to me on multiple levels. After all, the sense of self that had developed in me over the years was of being American rather than simply remaining Armenian.

Eventually, I decided to join the local Armenian club, as an important first step toward a discovery of what role Armenian-ness could play in my life. I didn't know what to expect when, one Saturday evening, I visited the place as an outside observer. While I was having a soft drink at the bar, I noticed that there were many Armenians from different countries and backgrounds, who mingled with each other in a friendly and relaxed atmosphere, having something in common to talk about. It was like one big Armenian family gathering, in one place, at one time.

On another occasion, I met a young man named Ara who was, like myself, Boston-born to Armenian immigrants. I introduced myself and our casual conversation touched on the Armenian community life. When he realized I knew so very little about Armenians, he said with a smile, 'They're an extraordinary people when you get to know them.'

'In what way?' I queried.

'We, Armenians, are hospitable people and family-oriented. We treat each other with kindness and courtesy but when it comes to helping a fellow Armenian reach his goal we don't want to get involved.'

'Why?' I wondered.

'This can be attributed to indifference or lack of sympathy,' Ara explained. 'You see, we're inherently jealous people. We cannot accept the idea that another Armenian is better than ourselves so we work hard to surpass others at all costs.'

'Jealousy is part of human nature,' I said.

'Yes, but it plays a dominant role in our character and sometimes leads to the downfall of a fellow Armenian.'

I put this question to him, 'How would you describe an Armenian as an individual?'

'In general, he's hard-working; clever when it comes to negotiating, hot-tempered and emotional when things go wrong, and sometimes a creative genius. Armenians are very successful individually, but not collectively.'

'Oh, why is that?' I asked in surprise.

'Because they're self-opinionated, trying to impose their views on one another about some project and, eventually, they find it too hard to come to a mutual understanding and give up.'

'Perhaps they find it easier to do business with foreigners rather than with one of their own,' I said.

'They'd prefer to do so, showing more tolerance towards foreigners. In general, an Armenian uses success for selfish personal reasons, but a Jew works for the benefit of their community while maintaining ethnic integrity.'

'They're mostly involved in charitable causes, that's an old Jewish tradition,' I added.

'One more thing; the new generation of diaspora Armenians and those local Armenians coming straight from Armenia don't get along.'

'What is the reason for this?' I asked.

'A clash of mentalities, customs and values, and also the difficulty in understanding the spoken version of the other, due to a difference in dialects. History will show you we've been a deeply divided nation, culturally and politically. The government of Armenia and the diaspora leaders have made a joint effort to bridge the gap on all issues but no breakthrough yet.'

Despite some misgivings, I found myself slowly drawn into the Armenian community. The following week, I began to browse the internet to learn more about Armenia and Armenians. My search led me to a history website, which put me in the picture about an ancient people from the land of myths and legends, to the rise and fall of their kingdoms and "Sea to Sea" empire over centuries of struggles, persecution and bloodshed.

In the evenings and weekends, for the first time in my life, I spent time researching and reading about Armenia. I figured out that there was once indeed a homeland called Turkish Armenia, which was situated in what is now central and eastern parts of Turkey, where about two million Armenians were living, over one million having been deported and exterminated by the Ottoman Turks in 1915. There were horrifying photos online, of gruesome suffering and death, which haunted me for the whole week. I saw blackened corpses strewn along the sides of roads, decapitated heads of Armenian victims, emaciated bodies of young women and starving children, looking like skeletons before they died.

Another article revealed that the Armenian Genocide was engineered by the Young Turks; a syncretist Jewish-Muslim sect which included Talaat Pasha, Enver Pasha,

Jemal Pasha, Behaeddin Shakir and Nizam Bey. Prior to that, there had also been massacres of Armenians in the mid-1890s, with estimates of the dead ranging from 100,000 to 300,000. Sultan Abdul Hamid II, who reasserted Pan-Islamism as a state ideology, was responsible for the butchery.

I gathered that the history of Armenia was one of tragedy, humiliation and loss. It was upsetting to learn about these forgotten mass atrocities and massacres, to which the big powers had turned a blind eye. I realized then why my father had wanted to raise me as an Armenian; to keep alive their struggle for justice. He also feared for my assimilation if I broke away from my roots. He had taken me aside one day, placed both his hands on my shoulders, and stared deeply into my eyes. 'Son; it would be a crime to deny your Armenian ethnicity,' he said. That was just a few weeks before he died.

From my conversation with a middle-aged Armenian named Zaven, who I had also met in the club, I figured out that the Armenians' struggle for justice was included in "The Armenian Cause", which embodied a series of causes and issues, the Armenian Genocide being a key element. There were three policy objectives: recognition that the 1915 events constituted a genocide; reparations from Turkey; restitution of the eastern provinces of Turkey to Armenia. I wondered if there was still sense in seeking justice for a cause that had been dragging on for 100 years. Then two questions came into my mind: Why had the Armenians been subjected to such horrible, inhuman and degrading treatment? What had they done to be cast out of their land?

Zaven had the answers. He said the Turks, or their

Ottoman ancestors, to be more exact, saw the Armenians as a threat when some of them revolted against the government; others had collaborated with the Russians during World War I, but he added that this was only a pretext to rid Turkey of Armenians forever. As for my second question, he said that there was a premeditated plan to annihilate the Armenian population in Asia Minor, in order to take their land.

At home, as a result of an internet search, I read about a major earthquake on 7 December 1988, which had devastated the northern region of the Soviet Armenian Republic, resulting in 25,000 deaths and leaving thousands homeless. Another article highlighted the bloody conflict of Nagorno-Karabakh, for which the Armenian name was "Artsakh". This was a landlocked enclave of predominantly ethnic Armenians, in the mountainous region of a southern neighbouring country, Azerbaijan, which had claimed the area as its own although in reality it belonged to the Armenians.

Despite all the tragedies – foreign domination, genocide, natural disaster – that struck the Armenian people over the centuries, they had survived and rebuilt their lives wherever they found refuge. The Armenian diaspora or the "victim diaspora" was estimated to be eight to ten million and its formation had resulted from the loss of their historical lands. It took the genocide survivors decades to organize themselves and establish schools, churches, cultural centres and enterprises. But the split within the diaspora itself affected relations both within communities and between the diaspora as a whole and the new Republic of Armenia.

My occasional visits to the club changed my life and my way of thinking about Armenians, who had both positive and negative sides. It was as if I was thrown into a new world, which was very different from my own; once far away and now close to me. During this time, I had been able to improve my Armenian, which I had spoken very little of before. As I became increasingly familiar with Armenian issues and gained a general grasp of their history from the internet, I found myself caught between two worlds, two different realities, two conflicting sets of values: mainstream American and ethnic Armenian.

# Chapter 2

It all happened unexpectedly one morning in the autumn of 2016. I was assigned by the newspaper's management to prepare myself for a visit to Armenia. They were aware of my ethnic origin and wanted me to find out all about this old and new country and write about my experiences. I was eager and excited to be travelling there; a real adventure and exploration awaited. The management did all the planning, booking my accommodation and aeroplane ticket, all expenses paid. In the evening I called my American fiancée to inform her about my trip. I said I would be back soon.

The following day, I set off at noon on the long journey to the free, distant homeland, which had been no more than a dream to me. Armenia was a self-isolated state of the South Caucasus region, between the Black Sea and Caspian Sea, exactly at the crossroads of Europe and Asia. It was once considered to be a unique trade centre, which connected the Eastern continent to the Western continent. During that period, Armenia fell under the influence of different ancient cultures and civilizations in the region.

The foreign invasions played a significant role in the cultural development of Armenia. Some typical Armenian traditions had faded away with time, some of them had survived till our day, and some of them had been replaced by others. Whether the Armenian people had been native to the Armenian highlands or immigrated there, presumably from the Balkans, they had existed for more than four thousand years and called themselves "*hay*", and their country "*Hayastan*".

It was just before midnight when my plane landed at Zvartnots International airport in Yerevan. Having gone through passport control, I hired a taxi. On the way to the hotel, I was greeted by a string of Vegas-like casinos, shining with colourful neon lights on either side of the street. After about ten minutes, the cab driver pulled over at my city-centre hotel. He looked at the taximeter and asked for 2000 Drams (about four US Dollars). I paid my fare and made my way into the hotel; a quiet place with a deserved reputation for good looks and warm hospitality. I reported to the reception desk and the bellboy carried my luggage up into a cosy single room which was equipped with all the necessary facilities, including access to the internet. I flopped down onto the bed, exhausted after a night of little sleep.

The next morning, after breakfast, I asked the lady at the reception desk to arrange a private tour guide for me; someone who could also speak English. She said she would deal with my request immediately and I sat in the lobby just in front, waiting for my guide. After fifteen minutes or so, a young man of about thirty years old walked in, towards the reception lady, who spoke to him and indicated me with a nod. He turned and saw me then came over to my seat.

He had thick black hair and was wearing jeans, a blue shirt and black shoes. I got to my feet to greet him.

'Hello, my name is Rouben Gabrielian, I'm your tour guide. Welcome to Armenia, Mr Bedrossian,' he said amiably, pausing to shake my hand. 'Hope you had a nice trip.'

'Yes, I did.'

'Is this your first time in Armenia?'

'Yes, and I have a question, actually.'

'Sure, what's that?'

'Am I allowed to take pictures inside the museums?'

'That's prohibited, but you can take pictures of the outside of the buildings. Shall we go?'

I nodded.

Together, we came out of the hotel and he guided me to his car.

'By the way, I speak English and Armenian, of course,' he reminded me with a smile.

'That suits me fine,' I said.

I got into his car and he drove off. 'Where do you come from?' he asked.

'Boston.'

He flicked a glance at me, 'How long will you be staying in Armenia?'

'Two weeks.'

'You don't have to go far from here to hit the most popular attractions,' he said. 'Almost everyone who comes to Armenia visits the Temple of Garni, which is out of the city, so I've got it first on my list.'

'OK, how long does it take to get there?'

'Oh, about forty minutes.'

After about fifteen minutes, Rouben asked, 'Would you

like to hear some Armenian popular music?'

'I don't mind if I do.'

He turned the car radio on and music came through – a fusion of traditional Armenian instruments and lyrics. We left the city and suburbs for the rural country and I marvelled at the landscape as we passed through hundreds of acres of highland pastures with barren mountains in the background.

Half turning toward me, Rouben smiled. 'It's beautiful, isn't it?'

'Yes, I'd never imagined being able to visit such remote places.'

A large blue sign along the main highway pointed the way to the temple. After passing through the village of Garni, Rouben stopped the car. 'We're nearly there!'

We got out and walked along the wide, stony path, at the end of which the Garni temple stood alone, at the edge of a triangular cliff and against a spectacular backdrop. As we approached the site, surrounded by the Caucasus mountains, Rouben recounted, 'This reconstructed pagan temple is one of the most ancient monuments of Armenia to have survived widespread destruction. It was built by King Trdat in the first century AD and dedicated to the sun god, Mihr. In 1679, a big earthquake left it in ruins but restoration of the temple began in 1966.'

I paused for a moment, gazing agape at the site. 'It reflects the architecture of the Greco-Roman style of temples,' I said.

'That's right,' Rouben confirmed.

'It's amazing how well preserved the temple is after being in existence for more than 2000 years.'

'Our government takes care of the maintenance of all

sites,' he said.

The temple was a rectangular building, surrounded on all sides by an open peristyle of Ionic columns. We walked past the remains of a Roman bathhouse, also nicely preserved. Having bought our entry tickets, we climbed wide steps leading to the temple's inner sanctum, passing between the six high columns at the front. The Arabic inscription at the entrance informed us about the capture of the fortress and the temple being turned into a mosque for some time. We made our way into the temple, which was, to my surprise, a medium-sized, empty room. Its walls were made of solid basalt blocks.

I looked around to find something of particular interest when Rouben said, 'It is believed that ancient pagan Armenians worshipped here many cults, some animals and fire, in order to keep spirits away. They sacrificed humans to honour their own gods…'

Rouben's voice faded out as my mind transported me back to pre-Christian times, with vivid mental images of worshippers wearing dark tunics and jewellery, gathering inside and outside the temple. As the priest came to perform the ceremony, fires were kindled from which someone would light a lantern to bring into the temple. I could hear the rising voices as they celebrated the ancient holy days and their heritage. Standing among the worshippers, my attention was absorbed in watching these people's customs and traditions. While the scenes of the ceremonies engulfed me, Rouben's voice began to intrude on my thoughts, addressing me twice in a low tone. 'Mr Bedrossian … Mr Bedrossian.'

I saw my guide staring at me.

'Is everything okay?' he asked, smiling.

'Sure,' I said.

When we got out, I took a snap of the temple, using my mobile phone, then we headed back towards his car.

'Like all pagan people,' Rouben said, 'Armenians believed in the spirits of nature and, after many years – perhaps centuries – they passed from nature worship to idol worship. Later on, they adopted key aspects of the Persian Zoroastrian belief that man is responsible for his acts.'

'Is pagan influence still felt in Armenia today?' I asked.

'That's a good question. Well, there are some people who keep the so-called ancient pagan traditions but in reality they're not pagans. Each year, a few hundred Armenians gather near the temple and celebrate Vartavar with traditional dances. This is also the day when kids and youngsters have great fun splashing buckets of water at one another in the streets of any village, town or city.'

'What does "Vartavar" mean?'

'The name comes from the Armenian word "Vart", meaning "rose", and is associated with the goddess of beauty and love, Astghik. According to tradition, the lady sprayed rose water as a symbol of love in Armenia. Many given names among Armenians today are the names of ancient gods and goddesses like Ara and Anahit.' Rouben started the car.

After several miles, I noted we were travelling a different route to the way we had come. 'Where're we going now?' I asked, curiously.

'To the Geghard monastery, it's only five miles on from Garni and it would be a pity to miss it when you are so close.'

We passed between rocky mountains before I caught sight of the monastery complex some distance away. Partly carved out of the cliff rocks, and beneath yellow crags, it was surrounded by high walls on three sides, with the mountain on the fourth. Upon arrival at the site, elderly women with gold-plated teeth warmly greeted visitors with baskets of freshly-baked sweet bread. Rouben and I followed the path leading to the monastery, which was lined with *khachkars* (rectangular stones engraved with ornate crosses and pagan botanic designs).

'According to tradition,' Rouben said, 'the monastery was founded in the fourth century by St Gregory, who was known as "the Illuminator". I will tell you about him later. Do you know what "Geghard" means?'

I shook my head.

'The holy lance that pierced Christ's side at the Crucifixion. It was later brought to Armenia by the Apostle Thaddeus, and since then it has been kept in the museum of Etchmiatzin Cathedral for centuries.'

The Geghard complex consisted of three interconnected chapels, with one entrance ornamented with carvings. As we stood outside the archway entrance to the main chapel, Rouben said, 'The chapel was built in 1215 by the Zakarians.' He pointed to the top of the doorway. 'That's the family emblem of a lion attacking an ox.'

I noticed there were some shallow shelves in the cliff. 'What are these for?' I asked.

'People throw pebbles onto them, to make their wishes come true.'

We went inside the secret rooms. One opened up into several smaller side rooms, filled with stone carvings of animals and crosses. I saw several tombs and a sacred spring flowing through one of the rooms.

'People take this water home in bottles, for its holy

properties,' Rouben said.

'Oh, I see.'

I saw a woman approaching the spring, holding a small bottle. She crossed herself and filled the bottle with the sacred water. When we went out, I noticed more *khachkars*, cut this time on rock surfaces and into the walls of the structures.

Back in the car, Rouben said, 'The site was originally named "Ayrivank", meaning "the monastery of the cave". It is included in the UNESCO World Heritage site list.'

He drove back towards the city and dropped me at the hotel.

# Chapter 3

Like the Jews, the Armenians had struggled for more than 4000 years to exist. According to Greek records and prominent ancient historians, the origins of the Armenians had been traced to prehistoric times (the Iron Age). Their oldest ancestors were the Hayasa-Azzi tribes, also known as Proto-Armenians, who lived in the native Armenian highlands in Eastern Anatolia. In the twelfth century BC, several other groups, of Thracian, Balkan and Phrygian tribes, along with the Armens, had crossed from Europe into Asia Minor. They eventually entered the Armenian plateau, absorbing more than a dozen tribes or races – like the Hayasa, Nairi, Khalds and Madiens - into their melting pot, resulting in a fusion of languages, traditions and cultures. Urartu, centred in Eastern Anatolia around Lake Van, became known as the Kingdom of Van, where the Armenian settlers inhabited the highlands surrounding the Biblical mountains of Ararat in what came to be their national home. The Urartians were then assimilated, becoming part of the Armenian ethnogenesis. Darius I (Darius the Great), in his famous Behistun Inscription, equated the two, saying that both were part of the same continuous entity. From then on, the names "Arminiya" and "Armenioi" began to appear in inscriptions and historical records. It was the beginning of an Armenian identity, with its Indo-European language, culture, and physical Aryan features. Armenia formally entered history while the memory of Urartu faded and finally disappeared.

Over the following centuries, Armenia was under the rule of different neighbouring and non-neighbouring countries and empires. The Armenians witnessed Alexander the Great's expeditions towards the east.

They fought the Roman legions and the Sassanid Persians, and in most cases lost. They stopped the Arabian expansion toward the north and provided emperors to the Byzantine throne. They fought against the invading Tartars and Seljuks in the eleventh century. The Cilician Armenian kingdom arose on the shores of the Eastern Mediterranean Sea, as a result of the mass immigration of Armenians from their original territory of Armenia to the west. Throughout those successive historical events, however, the Armenians struggled for their sovereignty and ruled locally from time to time. When everything seemed lost under foreign occupation, after a series of long battles would come the re-emergence of a new Armenian Royal Dynasty, state or kingdom, through some miracle of tenacious will and stubborn determination to survive.

The last battle of the early $20^{th}$ century was fought at Sardarabad, twenty miles away from the capital city Yerevan, against the advance of the third Ottoman army after the Bolshevik revolution (1917–1918) and the withdrawal of Russian troops from the Caucasus front. Poorly armed Armenian refugees and farmers gathered from what was left of a tattered Armenian nation and, forming a little ragtag army, fought back valiantly against the much larger Turkish army, which began a three-pronged attack in an attempt to capture all that remained of Armenia.

On 22 May 1918, the Armenian forces began repulsing the Ottoman advance and, over the next five days, miraculously saved the eastern heartland of Armenia from the Turks. On 28 May 1918, the First Republic of Armenia was formed. It enjoyed only two years of independence before it joined the Soviet sphere. The Armenian SSR, or Soviet Socialist Republic of Armenia, came into being on 29 November 1920. That period of existence was known as the Second Republic of Armenia and constituted only one-tenth of the historical Armenian plateau.

During the country's short-lived independence, Nakhichevan, a landlocked province south-west of Armenia, mostly populated by Armenians from ancient times, was the subject of a dispute between Armenia and Azerbaijan. The Armenian population largely fled the area during the Ottoman invasion but some of them returned to their homes a year later, after the British troops left the region. Nevertheless, more violence erupted, leaving 10,000 dead and some forty-five Armenian villages destroyed. Eventually, the treaty of Moscow was signed on 16 March 1921 and Nakhichevan, according to this treaty, became an autonomous territory under the auspices of Azerbaijan.

Armenia has a long, turbulent history and its mother tongue has suffered with its people. The tragic turn of historical events in the early 19th century, which resulted in the creation of a Russian Armenia and Turkish Armenia, and the Armenian Genocide a century later, divided the nation into two segments with two ideologies, two cultures, two churches, and two languages – Western and Eastern Armenian. After the establishment of Soviet rule in Armenia in late 1920, something like a cold war had surfaced amongst the entire Armenian diaspora. There were political factions in favour of communism, and those who were categorically opposed to this regime. During the global Cold War (1947–1991), these separate segments further deepened the historical differences between Soviet Armenia and the many Armenian communities scattered across the world. As a result, the Armenian nation was badly affected by their own cold war, and the worldwide East-West ideological polarization had erected the Iron Curtain through Armenia as well.

# Chapter 4

My next day out with Rouben began with a journey south-west from Yerevan towards the monastery of Khor Virap, the most visited pilgrimage site in Armenia.

'What does "Khor Virap" mean?' I asked with interest.

'"Deep dungeon"; it's the underground prison cell where St Gregory was imprisoned before he founded the Geghard monastery, remember?' Rouben said as we moved out of the city and onto the highway. After half an hour's drive, he pointed to Mount Ararat and said, 'Look there!'

I crouched a little and saw the real mountain as my memory flashed back for a few seconds to its painted picture which hung in our Boston house.

'You can see it from all parts of Yerevan in clear weather,' Rouben went on, 'but it's much better to get a closer view of the mountain from up at the monastery.'

'Obviously,' I said.

After a short silence, he cast a glance at me. 'May I ask what you do for a living?'

'I'm a journalist.'

'That's an interesting career. I assume you write your

articles in Armenian.'

I shook my head. 'No, in English.'

'Perhaps that is why you don't speak fluent Western Armenian.'

'Because I grew up outside the community,' I replied without elaboration.

It took us another quarter-hour to finally arrive in Khor Virap. Rouben left the car down the street and as we climbed the hill and reached the monastery, I caught sight of the majestic mountain looming on our left with its twin peaks and their eternal snows. It stood there real, alone in all its glory.

'I never saw anything so marvellous before,' I said. 'You know, when the mountain is so close, it appears like a huge, isolated structure, rising out of the plain and dominating the skyline.'

'That's the Biblical mountain that has figured in legends since time began. Tradition holds that Noah's Ark came to rest there after the great flood, and a portion of it is now displayed in the Etchmiatzin museum.' Pointing to the bottom of the mountain, Rouben continued, 'Can you see the wire fence along the Araks River?'

I took my small binoculars out of my bag and raised them to my eyes. 'Yes, I can see it clearly now.'

'That indicates the boundary with Turkey, there are several military lookout posts around the area. That noble mountain used to be ours,' he lamented, 'it is still a national symbol for the Armenian people.'

Rouben guided me to the Gevork chapel, which was a small basilica with a semi-circular apse. Inside, we moved through two unmarked holes into a small chamber where a winding stairway led to the prayer room. From there, a heavy iron ladder descended ten metres vertically, into a stone hole. We went down slowly through the gathering darkness until the ladder changed direction and came to an end near the middle of a circular room about fourteen-feet wide and dimly lit by a single electric lightbulb.

Rouben recounted, 'King Trdat put the Christians to death in pagan times and kept Gregory just here for fourteen years, guilty of preaching Christianity.'

'But how did he survive his incarceration?' I asked.

'Some people say God sent a devoted woman to feed him each day; others think it was not a woman but an angel of the Lord.'

As I looked around my attention was focused on a small hole high above in the roof and I pictured that scene in which a voice echoed through the hole, "Gregory … Gregory…" Suddenly, a single loaf soaked in water was dropped down with a thud. Rouben's voice came to me once more, addressing me. 'Mr Bedrossian...'

I pulled myself together and we climbed back up the ladder to the upper rooms. 'The pit down there,' Rouben said, 'was filled at the time with poisonous snakes and scorpions, but God protected Gregory.'

I looked sidelong at him. 'Oh, that's scary for anyone who wants to visit the pit.'

'One day,' he resumed the tale, 'King Trdat fell seriously ill and his sister had a vision where an angel told her that Gregory could heal her brother. The people believed he would have died a long time ago. To everyone's amazement, he was pulled out of the pit alive and cured the king, who converted to Christianity and had the entire kingdom do the same.'

'That's really amazing.'

We exited the chapel and began our walk down the hill, Rouben concluding, 'Thus, Armenia became the first officially Christian nation in 301 AD. Since then, Gregory's story was hailed as a miracle and he was called "the Illuminator". Locals come to this holy site for a baptism or a sacrifice.'

Back in the car, Rouben thought for a moment then said, 'Would you like to visit the Noravank monastery? This is something you definitely do not want to miss, whatever you plan to see in Armenia.'

'How far is it?'

'It takes one-and-a-half hours from here.'

'That's a long way off. Is there a restaurant there so we can eat something?' I asked.

'There's one near to the monastery,' he said.

'Okay then, this is the chance of a lifetime.'

He drove off and we re-entered the highway, Rouben accelerating. 'You said you're a journalist. What type of articles do you write?' he asked.

'I cover all kinds of news stories, mainly political.'

'Do you also conduct interviews?'

'Yes, of course.'

'In your view, what are the qualities today that make a good journalist?'

'He or she must be resourceful, trustworthy and tenacious,' I said.

He shot a glance at me. 'May I ask why you chose this career?'

'Well, watching the evening news every day made me think I'd get the biggest thrill, covering all the exciting news stories.'

'How much work do you think is put into reporting?'

'A lot, especially when it comes to breaking news,' I said.

As Rouben drove on, we passed by a "stork village"; rows of long poles lined the road, hosting a great number of storks' nests at their crests. 'These storks migrate to Africa in the winter and come back in spring,' he said.

After a further forty kilometres to the south, we reached Noravank, which was situated in a narrow gorge and encircled by red rocks. Rouben parked the car and we climbed the steep, narrow stairs which led to the site.

'The monastery was built in the 13th century and it was used as a residence for Armenian bishops,' he said. 'One of them, Stepanos Orbelian, turned it into a cultural and religious centre.'

The monastery complex included three churches, the first being St Astvatsatsin: the Church of the Holy Mother of God. The semi-circular tympanum of the entrance to the church had a relief showing the icon of the blessed Virgin with baby Christ and two saints facing her. In the corners of the inner framing there were four sirens and birds with crowned human heads.

'Most of this sculptural work was done by Momik, a prominent artist who was brought to Armenia by Bishop Stepanos,' Rouben explained.

The lower relief depicted an enthroned Holy Virgin with the Christ child in her lap, flanked by the archangels Gabriel and Michael. The upper relief carving depicted Christ, flanked by Saints Peter and Paul. Christ was holding a tablet, his right index finger and middle finger extended in a sign of blessing.

'The artist has worked on his craft so skilfully he was able to project his figures from the stone,' I said.

The two other churches in the Noravank complex were

that of St Stepanos and the adjoining small basilica of St Garabed. A series of earthquakes in the past had damaged much of the dome of the former, which was rebuilt at least twice, and the latter was still in ruins, fragments of Momik's carved stone crosses paving the ground.

We went down to a modest restaurant where the waiter seated us next to the window. The menu on the table included traditional Armenian dishes such as stuffed aubergines with vegetables and *sarma* (meat, rice, onions and herbs wrapped in fresh vine leaves). We went for the latter, which was particularly good.

'What is most striking is that these monasteries and churches are all located in the middle of beautiful landscapes,' I said.

'Oh, there are so many historical sites in this country that you need at least a year or two to visit them all.'

'I think the most popular ones will be enough for me,' I said.

'One of them is the ancient Tatev monastery but it is in the south of the country and takes four to five hours to get there. It stands on the edge of a deep gorge; a breath-taking view.'

'Well, it would be nice to visit the place if we have time. When was it built?' I asked.

'In the ninth century. According to legend, during the construction of the church an apprentice secretly climbed to the top of its steeple to place a cross. When spotted by his master on his descent, he lost his foothold and cried out, "Let the holy spirit give me the wings." Hardly had he said so when two wings grew on his back and he flew away. So the monastery got the name "Tatev", meaning "wing".'

'Quite interesting, I'll see what more I can find out about

that on the internet.'

After lunch, we left the restaurant and Rouben drove me back to my hotel as I felt very sleepy. We arranged to meet in the lobby at ten the next morning.

# Chapter 5

Rouben came to the hotel at the appointed time. Once we were in his car and on our way, he turned onto a street called Amirian. 'Look,' he said, indicating the luxurious hotels, open-air cafés and fashionable boutiques, 'none of these places ever existed in Soviet times.' Further ahead, he pointed to the left side of the road and went on, 'The old house on the corner there will be taken down, to be replaced by a modern building.'

'There are street beggars over there,' I said, gesturing towards them.

'They too didn't exist before. I suppose there are also beggars in Boston?'

'Of course, there's no country without them.'

'Some people here are complaining these days and feel they were happier in the past because there was no unemployment or homelessness, and no beggars, in their country. Even crimes and robberies were much less frequent, and education and medical care were free. Today, more and more local Armenians want to emigrate,' Rouben explained.

'I'm sorry they've decided to leave their homeland,' I said.

'They would say there's nothing to do in Armenia. No proper money, no proper living, no progress. The people here are nervous and don't smile often because of an uneasy life,' Rouben shrugged.

'Life abroad is not as rosy as they think.'

Rouben drove the car around the Republic Square - a large oval roundabout. 'Ceremonies and meetings are held here; the most notable one is the annual military show of Independence Day,' he said. 'The building behind the fountains is the history museum, where you can find a huge collection of objects from Stone Age to modern times, I'll take you there one day.'

'By all means,' I said.

'The square is surrounded mostly by ministry and government buildings, and the Marriott Hotel, in the best traditions of Armenian architecture. It was once called Lenin Square and had a statue of Lenin, which was removed from there,' he pointed to the stretch of grass that had replaced the statue.

I gave a nod of approval and said, 'Looks like a modern European city with its wide streets, subways, big parks, malls, new and old buildings between monuments and museums.'

'Yerevan long ago became known as the Pink City, due to the colour of the stone used for building. It is also the City of Lights at night. You could spend hours just aimlessly walking along the streets or sitting on a bench and looking at the new world around you.'

Rouben turned left at the junction and drove on then pulled over. He pointed to the statue erected at the centre of a memorial square. 'That's Vartan Mamikonian, charging on a horse, with a sword in his right hand. He was a military commander, a martyr and a saint of the Armenian Church.'

'Whose work is it?' I asked.

'Yervand Kochar, a prominent painter and sculptor.'

'Good monument, what story does it tell?' I asked, for I didn't recall having read about this hero and saint.

'In the mid fifth century the Persian ruler, King Yazdigert II, who was particularly cruel to Armenians, demanded the renunciation of their religion and the submission to the precepts of the pagan Persian religion. Ultimately, Vartan was forced to fight, along with his soldiers, against the more powerful and larger Persian army, to defend their Christian faith. Vartan himself was killed but this turned out to be a moral victory for the Armenians as the Persians gave up their efforts to assimilate them.'

'Oh, they definitely stood firm to maintain their religious freedom.'

Rouben then took Mashtots Avenue and drove north. 'I'm taking you now to the Matenadaran – a unique research institute and the museum of ancient manuscripts,' he said.

After a short while, Rouben parked the car near the slope leading to the museum. There was a group of pastry shops and on the opposite corner was the shop of Grand Candy, with the adjacent doughnut café. 'Look up there now,' he said as he stopped, pointing to a monument of a lady that stood alone upon a hill in the distance. Arms raised almost to chest height, she was holding a huge sword in both hands, across her body.

I surveyed the statue as Rouben continued, 'That's Mother Armenia, rising forty-three metres in height and made of 8000 tons of hammered copper. It can be seen from any angle and any high building in Yerevan.'

'An imposing sight,' I said. 'It makes her look like a wide-awake guardian of the city, ready to lash out and attack.'

'That was precisely the aim of the monument's creation,' Rouben said. 'It stands within the Victory Park, where there are various fairground amusements and a boating lake.'

A little further ahead, we paused in front of the institute at the statue of Mesrop Mashtots and his student kneeling beside him. 'Mesrop was the inventor of the Armenian alphabet, in 406 AD, and laid the foundation of Armenian culture, thus he saved his nation from impending moral and physical destruction. He and his students translated the Holy Bible into Armenian,' Rouben told me.

'What was the source language being translated?'

'Greek. According to our historians, St Mesrop had a vision where an angel came down and marked the Armenian alphabet on his chest. Tradition also tells us that when he was deeply meditating to find the vowels of the alphabet, a luminous hand wrote them on the wall.'

'Fascinating,' I said.

We climbed a flight of steps leading up to the institute, which was named after the saint. In front of the entrance stood sculptures of the great thinkers, scientists and cultural figures of ancient times – Toros Roslin and Grigor Tatevtsi, amongst others. We went inside the museum, where original and hand-written copies of more than 20,000 old manuscripts were on display in the halls, full of elaborate miniatures, carefully preserved. Sadly, tens of thousands of other manuscripts have been destroyed over the years, in the countless wars and invasions of the country.

There was a fine archive department which had more than 100,000 documents, in Armenian and various other languages, belonging to the 14th–19th centuries. These documents contained a wealth of material on the history of the political and socio-economic life of Armenia and neighbouring countries.

We paused to look at one of the oldest preserved manuscripts, entitled *The Book of Lamentations*, by St Gregory of Narek, a devoted Christian who composed prayers for saving souls and whose inspired writings had taken their place as jewels in the rites of the Armenian Church.

'In ninety-five prayers, Narek translated the sighs of the heart into an offering of words pleasing to God,' Rouben told me gently, 'and the result was an edifice of faith and its sincere communication with God.'

As we made our way out of the institute, he asked, 'Did you know that Pope Francis officially proclaimed Gregory a Doctor of the Church?'

'I heard that last year.'

Born in 951 AD, St Gregory entered Narek Monastery on the southern shore of Lake Van, in what is now eastern Turkey. He came from a line of scholars and churchmen and went through his daily ritual of studying the Bible during the Armenian Renaissance, which flourished with art, literature, architecture and theology. Dedicating himself to God, he lived most of his life in the monastery and wrote many *sharagans*, melodies, odes, and discourses. He was a monk of many talents – poet, philosopher, mystic theologian, and, above all, a devotee after God's own Heart.

The *Book of Prayer*, which he called his last testament, was the work of his mature years. It was his hope that it would serve as a complete guide to prayer for all the people in the world. St Gregory plumbed the depths of his heart in search of God's loving truth. Like the *Confessions*, his book of prayer was an expression of the universal human search for reconciliation with the divine, translating the pure sighs of the "broken and contrite" heart into an offering acceptable to God.

'King on high, mighty and awesome,
blessed Lord Jesus Christ,
for someone like me who despairs of salvation
only you can change the curse of mortality
into the blessing of life.
Only you can turn the discouragement of blame
into joyous praise,
shame into resilience,
humility into honour,
banishment into the hope of goodness,
separation into the expectation of reunion,
menacing words into compassionate comfort,
final condemnation into a second chance
at deliverance.' (Prayer 73a)

Through his work, St Gregory turned the inexpressible, sometimes indefinable, thoughts and feelings of humans into beautiful, earnest words of prayer. He lamented not his plight but his unworthiness of God's grace and his own ingratitude and disobedience in the face of God's will. The experience of grace was expressed vividly, in a variety of metaphorical images. Using parabolic language, he made the obscure clear, the ineffable expressible, and the unknown graspable. Some of his prayers had the flavour of proverbial wisdom and offered counselling for a good life. He praised the infinite goodness and power of God.

'What is impossible for me is easy for you.
What is beyond my reach is grasped by you.
What is hidden for me in my fallen state
is within view for your supreme goodness.
What is undoable for me is done by you.' (Prayer 57a)

'In the face of my evil, you are good.
In the face of my total indebtedness, you are forgiving.
In the face of my sinfulness, you are indulgent.
In the face of my darkness, you are light.
In the face of my mortality, you are life.' (Prayer 58b)

St Gregory linked himself with the *Book of Prayer* and, ever since, the book has been equated with this saintly man. So the book, like the man, came to be known affectionately as "Narek"; written in the last years of his life when he appears to have been suffering from a debilitating terminal illness. Toward the end he wrote, "and although I shall die in the way of all mortals, may I be deemed to live through the continued existence of this book. This book will cry out in my place, with my voice, as if it were me."

So powerfully had these prayers cried out to the Armenian faithful that for centuries they had been placed under the pillows of the infirm as healing talismans.

Narek noted in his prologue that the book was designed to be an applied synthesis of theology and worship for the spiritual development of ordinary Christians and monastics the world over. The Armenian people considered his work a masterpiece of intuitive and direct communion with God. According to tradition, St Gregory saw God, to whom he gave witness in his prayers, where he truly regretted his wrongdoing. The monk also testified that the book, an "edifice of faith", was written by the hand of God and it was his second attempt to compose the book: "I destroyed with my own hand the golden tables of speech, dedicated to your message, and now, with ashen-faced sorrow, I provide a second copy, made in its likeness."

# Chapter 6

Over the centuries, Armenians had been a subjugated people, with no independent state. In seventy years under communism, they experienced yet more pain and suffering in a so-called just and communal society, and any attempt at revolt could have led to one's disappearance. After the collapse of the Soviet Union, Armenia was one of the first republics to declare independence, on 21 September 1991. That independence, however, was thrust on her as a consequence of the dissolution of the Soviet regime. A sizeable proportion of the population was not ready to embrace independence, which happened against their wishes, because decades of dependency on communist leadership had rendered them incapable of suddenly having to govern a new, free country with no support.

A year later, the state of Armenia was re-established and became known as the Third Republic of Armenia.

The first years of independence brought economic and financial ruin to the landlocked country, leaving it helpless. The large industrial complexes were abandoned or sold.

The high levels of resultant unemployment led to masses of young, skilled Armenians seeking work elsewhere. Since then, many wealthy diaspora Armenians have been helping Armenia to survive, through donations. The Armenia Fund, which was established in 1992 in Los Angeles, is a non-profit and non-political organization dedicated to supporting large-scale, self-sustaining initiatives in both Armenia and Karabakh. The fund is primarily focused on building sustainable infrastructure for the region, through the development of roads, schools, medical facilities and utilities. Additionally, the fund has invested in humanitarian programmes, education, training and healthcare.

Although there have been improvements in the lives of the local people, the overall results have been extremely disappointing; the greedy oligarchs, including government officials, continued to prosper, enjoying a lavish lifestyle, while levels of poverty significantly increased in the general population.

Corruption had been a defining characteristic of Armenian politics. It remained a significant obstacle in areas such as judiciary, health, education, public procurement, tax/customs operations, and even social benefits. As a result, the whole economy and much of the population suffered. Anti-corruption mass protests had been on the rise, drawing people to the streets to campaign against rampant corruption among the authorities and the government's ubiquitous lack of transparency. Despite successive governments' promises to deal with the problem, and anti-corruption councils being set up, too little had changed. There was a large "under the table" economy and a lot of economic activity was not recorded or reported. People worked side jobs, got kickbacks, or were simply corrupt and all the while most of the working families were struggling to make ends meet.

I met an Armenian student in a café. He had long since considered himself to be a local. He had spent more than eight years studying in a local university, worked in different organizations, and tried out being self-employed. He felt deeply the imbalance between salary and the cost of living and showed me in numbers in a convenient little table how that imbalance played out. I saw the huge disparity; the cost of minimum survival in this country was about three times more than the average income. He didn't even include things like clothing, eating out with friends, or leisure activities, and excluded the inevitable and expensive medical fees.

Looking at the average monthly salary, which was $200 - and many people made a lot less - I thought to myself that it was wrong. He said there were only a handful of professionals who earned salaries far beyond the average. In fact, there was huge social injustice. When I asked the student how these people were surviving, the categorical answer was – remittances. A great number of Armenian citizens worked in Russia, most of them bringing sufficient income to support their families in Armenia. But still, I wondered if those Armenians working abroad in major cities, with a high cost of living, could really afford remittances.

I found out that the diaspora and local Armenians had experienced the bitter contrast between the "Armenian dream" of decent living, a bright future and success, and the grim realities of poverty, rampant corruption, unemployment, and emigration.

Still, despite the hardships locals had been through, they remained sociable, friendly, hospitable and generous people, with a sense of humour. I had latched onto this phrase several times in a day: "*Tsavt Danem*", meaning "let me take your pain on me". I kept asking myself how anyone except our Lord could take or feel another person's pain. Although the expression was often used in an emotional and affectionate way, sometimes expecting a favour in return, and at other times after bad news or expressing love, I realized that it was a cliché rather than a consolation.

I had noticed for some time that the locals used many Russian and other foreign words in their everyday speech. I overheard the word "*marojni*", and figured out that it meant ice cream. When I met a diaspora Armenian in my hotel's lobby and asked him the reason for using these foreign words, he said, 'They're easy to pronounce for them. The Armenian spoken here differs much from ours in vocabulary and syntax, as well as in the spelling and pronunciation. Diaspora Armenians and local Armenians are having some, if not many, difficulties understanding each other. Our Western Armenian language sounds ridiculous to them, and vice versa.'

'You're right,' I said, 'I'm having myself trouble understanding these native Armenians. It feels as if you need to bring a translator.'

He laughed, 'I think an extended stay in this country would probably fix the problem for a diasporan Armenian.'

'In fact, history deserves the blame for the division of the Armenian language. Doesn't the government here have a plan to include the Western Armenian language on the school curriculum?' I asked.

'It's currently taught at several universities in Armenia. There are also summer language courses.'

'But there must be some kind of convergence of the two languages; it's hard to imagine a nation without a common national language.'

Over the last two decades, the division of the language has created confusion, particularly among the diaspora Armenian pupils, and raised questions in their minds; why two Armenian languages? Which one to learn? The one practised in today's Armenia or the one in the diaspora?

Although Western Armenian has continued to be used by the diaspora, it has declined sharply over the years, to the extent that UNESCO had placed it on the list of endangered languages, if serious initiatives were not undertaken to reinforce it. There have been significant changes in the way the new generation of diaspora Armenians grasp their ethno-cultural identity, along with considerable differences with regard to feelings of loyalty to their mother tongue, homeland and heritage.

To one segment of the Armenians, the fact that their ancestors were Armenian a century ago had no significance. They would say, 'After all, we weren't born in Armenia, why should we feel and speak Armenian?'

They wanted to move on with their lives and use the first national language in their respective host countries, for they thought Armenian a useless language and "*Hay Thad*" (the Armenian Cause) a hopeless cause.

To another segment of diasporans, it was important to keep their cultural heritage and feel Armenian rather than to be Armenian.

# Chapter 7

Rouben called me at the hotel and said he would pick me up in fifteen minutes. I came down from my room and waited for him outside the entrance to the hotel. A few minutes later, he pulled his car over in front of me and I got in.

He cast a look at me and smiled. 'How're you?'

'Fine, where're we going today?'

'To the Freedom Square, a great place to visit for anyone who wants to learn more about Armenian culture.'

He turned onto Mashtots Avenue and after a short while he drove into an underground parking lot, beneath Freedom Square. We left the car there, climbing a couple of flights of stairs to the square, where Rouben guided me towards two large statues in front of the oval opera building.

As we paused at one of them, Rouben said, 'This is Alexander Spendiaryan, a composer and conductor, and the founder of Armenian National Symphonic music. The opera theatre was named after him and many great performances have been given there.'

We drew near to the other statue, on which the name of

Hovhannes Toumanian was inscribed. 'He's our national poet,' Rouben gestured to the statue, 'also a master of quatrains and fables.'

He recited, to my surprise, one of Toumanian's poems, revealing the inner world of the poet:

> Armenian grief is a sea,
> A fathomless, boundless main.
> In that dark expanse drifts my soul,
> Mournful, in mortal pain.
> Now furiously it rears
> And the azure coastline seeks,
> Now weary it disappears,
> Seeking peace in the deeps.
> But neither can it find the bottom,
> Nor can it reach the shore…
> In the sea of Armenian sorrows
> My soul languishes evermore.

'It's beautiful and sentimental,' I said.

A flush of pride crept across Rouben's face, 'I'm sure you've heard of Paruyr Sevak, Vahan Terian, and Yeghishe Charents?'

He started to bug me with the names of other poets. Shaking my head in annoyance, I said, 'No, the Armenians have the right of course to admire their great poets, writers, composers, and musicians, but most of them are virtually unknown outside the Armenian communities.'

He stared at me in disbelief. 'What about William Saroyan, who writes his novels in English?'

'Haven't heard of him either. I'm sure people have heard much more of Charles Dickens or William Shakespeare.'

We strolled through the square. There was a large pond, which was surrounded by many open-air cafés, restaurants and ice cream stalls. The gardens were clean and colourful.

'Nice place to walk,' I said.

'After Independence, the square was the main location of anti-government rallies and sit-ins, but they passed off without serious trouble.'

'Let's have a cup of coffee,' I suggested.

We sat at a vacant table on the terrace and Rouben summoned a waiter, who took our order.

'I hear there are numerous political parties in this country,' I said.

He nodded in agreement, 'Oh, more than a hundred since Independence, but only a dozen or so have had electoral success.'

'That is far too many for a small country like Armenia. They should consider uniting around three or four main parties.'

'New alliances have been formed lately and opposition parties came together to form blocks ahead of elections. The thing is, sometimes we become hot-headed, and evidence of that shows up during election campaigns and parliamentary sessions.'

The waiter delivered two cups of coffee to our table.

'What is surprising is that the ruling Republican party lacks political ideology, which is not the case in the US,' I said.

Rouben's eyes glinted, 'What's the use of being ideological in a country where the electoral system doesn't work well, and where the three pillars of the government are all under the direct control of oligarchs?'

'Well, you cannot do much under the circumstances.'

Rouben sipped his coffee and said, 'I also hear the Armenian diaspora is disorganised, with diverse views.'

'One should talk about communities of not just one but several diasporas. There are only appointed community leaders and not one leadership, and I think these people don't have the necessary skills to represent diaspora Armenians.'

'You're right,' he nodded.

'So, in my view, it's imperative to create a new structure that would represent Armenians worldwide and the elected representatives would have the right to speak on behalf of the diaspora with one voice. But the problem is, internal political division makes it difficult to develop a clear diasporic strategy.'

'There have been annual Armenia-Diaspora conferences held in Yerevan; how important are they, in your view?' Rouben asked.

'The elite local and diaspora Armenians don't see eye-to-eye on a vast number of issues,' I said. 'There's only consensus on a few items.'

'Pity, isn't it?'

'Diaspora representatives argue that no diaspora-born figures have held cabinet-level or other prominent positions in Armenia's government since 2008,' I said. 'What's the use then of keeping up the so-called "One nation, One homeland" slogan?'

'There's also "One nation, one culture" rhetoric propagated by our Ministry of the Diaspora,' Rouben replied.

'One culture? This is questionable,' I said. 'Anyway, diaspora Armenians love their homeland on the whole. The fact is, they've been donating generously to this country.'

'But people here say some of these donations have been channelled elsewhere, into the pockets of members of the government.'

'I don't think so; donors make sure the funds go to the right place,' I said and continued, 'Now, think what would have become of Armenia without the diaspora's help.'

After a moment of reflection, Rouben lamented, 'A backward third world nation.' He burst out, 'We don't need donations anymore, just a normal government that collects the correct taxes from all the oligarchs to restore justice and local confidence in our society. Unfortunately, those oligarchs continue to rule the country and go unpunished.'

'In Western countries, there is a special investigative commission that prosecutes any member of a government, including the president, for corruption, bribery, fraud, and misuse of state funds,' I said.

Rouben's brows knitted as he affirmed, 'There's no such thing here, never will be. The funny thing is, the government claims to take anti-corruption measures but they're the corrupt ones. Hypocrisy, isn't it? The fish rots from the head down.'

'That's why diasporan investors refrain from engaging fully in Armenia.'

'The frozen, dangerous conflict over Karabakh is another reason,' he reminded me.

I nodded. 'Shall we go?'

I took some coins from my pocket and slid them onto the table. As we headed back to the parking lot, we passed the State Conservatory. 'See there?' he said, pointing to another statue. 'That's Komitas, sitting on the trunk of a tree. He's the founder of Armenian classical music, and the conservatory was named after him.'

I looked at the monument while Rouben continued, 'His songs won a special place in the hearts of Armenians everywhere.'

Komitas rediscovered the pre-Christian roots of Armenian sacred music and brought its folk music to a high standard. He performed pieces fashioned from millennia-old material, which he had carefully polished and imbued with cultural and religious significance. The musician's countless heritages had presented great scientific and theoretical value in composition, musical ethnography and performing arts. As a result, his creative work had continuously been a particular focus of attention in Europe. It had become a source of inspiration for both Armenian and foreign contemporaries. He was the first non-European musicologist to join the International Musical Society, where he lectured on folk and sacred music, introducing the unique musical heritage of Eastern cultures to the West.

On 24 April 1915, which marked the beginning of the Armenian Genocide, Komitas was arrested, alongside more than 200 Armenian intellectuals and community leaders, and deported far inland by the Ottoman government. His behaviour changed along the exile route, after being physically abused. Although he survived the death camp with a few other notables, he developed Post Traumatic Stress Disorder (PTSD) and so ended his musical career. Having lost his mental and spiritual balance, he spent the last twenty years of his life in asylums and died in Paris, in 1935. The next year, his ashes were transferred to Yerevan and buried in the Pantheon, which was named after him. The music of Komitas, and the vast body of folk songs that he had collected, helped him secure over the decades a unique place in Armenian culture. He is remembered and revered as much by his people as by prominent musicians.

# Chapter 8

The Genocide Memorial was the next visit on Rouben's list. Driving towards the football stadium, a blue sign with white lettering indicated the route. After 100 yards or so, Rouben followed the road up the hill, until we reached the free parking lot just in front of the museum. The memorial complex was dedicated to the memory of the 1.5 million Armenians who perished between 1915 and 1922.

Inside the museum, the story of the horrific events was told through photographs, documents, newspaper reports and films – a shocking history of death and destruction. I noticed that some of the photos were the same as the ones I had seen on the internet, back in Boston. From the museum, a broad pathway flanked by a 100-metre-long wall and engraved with the names of massacred communities led us to the memorial, which consisted of an arrow-shaped forty-metre-high spire symbolizing the rebirth of the Armenian people. Nearby stood twelve basalt slabs, leaning inwards over an eternal flame, which memorialized all the victims of the Genocide. The tilted slabs represented the lost provinces of the former Western

Armenia after World War I.

We descended a flight of stairs, entered the inner space and walked solemnly toward the eternal flame. There we laid a red rose on its stone perimeter and bowed as a mark of respect to the victims of the Genocide.

While we observed a one-minute silence and I fixed my eyes on the flame, which grew bigger, taking up my entire field of vision, I was carried all the way back to the massacres. I heard screams of terror and pain as I saw, in successive mental images, men, women and children, slaughtered in cold blood by the Turkish soldiers. The tormenting sound of agonized cries of women filled my ears but a gentle voice interrupted my thoughts. It was Rouben, addressing me twice, 'Mr Bedrossian ... Mr Bedrossian...'

I was suddenly conscious of his hand holding my arm and he looked at me as I pulled myself together. 'Sorry,' I said, 'I was remembering what I've learned about the Genocide.'

'It will never fade away,' Rouben lamented. 'Shall we go?'

'Yes.'

We climbed back up the stairs and walked along the pathway towards his car. 'At normal times like now,' he went on, 'there are just a few flowers laid by the eternal flame but on 24 April, Genocide Commemoration Day, the place becomes flooded with flowers as hundreds of thousands of local and diaspora Armenians gather at the memorial.'

'Where do all the flowers go afterwards?' I asked.

'They're collected by volunteers for recycling, but some of them go to the waste.'

'Oh, I see.'

'It struck me one day that 24 April has been over the years commemorated during the month of Jesus's sufferings and resurrection. The fact that both events took place only a few weeks apart seems to be significant, doesn't it?' Rouben remarked.

'Yes, it does,' I said after a moment of reflection.

'A priest once told me that God wanted to show the world in time that our nation, the first to embrace Christianity, followed His son's example by suffering and dying for His sake during the Genocide.'

'Oh, brush it off.'

'How did you commemorate the centenary of the Genocide last year in Boston?'

'By going on a march and holding a protest at the Turkish consulate, but there were huge demonstrations elsewhere.'

'American presidents have failed to keep their campaign promise to call our tragedy a "genocide". They only used the words "*Mets Yeghern*", meaning "Great Calamity" in their annual commemorative statements. Don't you think this should be viewed as an acknowledgement of the Armenian Genocide?' Rouben asked.

'That is not a legal term and has no meaning for all non-Armenians. Secondly, I don't understand why those naïve Armenians desperately hope that the US president will use the words "Armenian Genocide" when it has already been recognized by forty-six US states and two House resolutions adopted.'

'President Reagan recognized it,' he said.

'What more do the Armenians want, then?' I said. 'I don't see any benefit in holding worldwide rallies every year to commemorate a genocide that happened a long time ago. I mean, what's the point? These would harm the

Armenian Cause.'

Upon reflection, Rouben nodded. 'You may be right.'

'I think the diaspora leaders, together with the government in Armenia, should try to resolve the issue through legal action and take it to the International Court of Justice,' I commented.

'But a recognition of the Genocide by the present regime in Turkey is extremely unlikely,' he observed.

Rouben took me back to the hotel and we ended another day.


Over the past century there have been many examples of crimes against humanity, which were carried out because of racial and/or religious prejudices and political schemes. These crimes employed methods such as deportation or forcible transfer of population; imprisonment; torture; enforced prostitution; slavery; death camps; secret police, and massacres.

The Armenian Genocide was one of many heinous crimes perpetrated against its people. Despite the stringency of the Turkish censorship of photography and reporting, many American missionaries and consuls residing in different parts of the empire bore witness to the mass deportations and massacres. The US Ambassador to Ottoman Turkey, Henry Morgenthau, acknowledged in a cable to the US Department that what was happening to the Armenians was "a campaign of race extermination".

By 1920, the bulk of the Armenian population had been eliminated from Asia Minor, in parallel with the confiscation and appropriation of all their properties. Although the three main perpetrators of this crime – Talaat, Enver, and Jemal Pashas - had been tried and sentenced to death by the Military Tribunal in Constantinople (now Istanbul), the sentence was not enforced and the criminals fled to Germany for safety.

Early in that year, a group of Armenians from the radical Armenian Revolutionary Federation had formed what became known as "Operation Nemesis", a covert operation to assassinate the three political leaders for their key role in organizing and implementing the massacres against the Armenians. The ARF, knowing that the crime couldn't remain unpunished, held their Ninth World Congress in Armenia and decided to carry out the assassination campaign for which diplomatic supporters succeeded in tracking down the Ottoman villains.

The first target in revenge for the Armenian Genocide was Talaat and it was Soghomon Tehlirian's mission to assassinate him. Tehlirian travelled to Germany to study and at the same time hunt for Talaat. In early March 1921 he found him in Berlin, hiding in a house located on Hardenberg Street. Tehlirian rented an apartment on the opposite side of the road to Talaat's house. On 15 March, seeing Talaat step outside, Tehlirian ran downstairs and crossed the street. He followed the old man and, passing him to confirm his identity, quickly pulled his revolver, turned round and shot Talaat at point-blank range, with a bullet through his head. The man fell dead instantly, in a pool of blood.

Tehlirian was arrested by the police on a charge of murder and faced trial by the German Court. The defendant told the story of his slaughtered family and of the Armenian Genocide, and justified his motives for retaliation. The trial ended with his acquittal, for he was seen as a man of equity and justice.

A year later, Enver and Jemal Pashas were assassinated by the Armenian revenge-takers, the former in Tajikistan and the latter in Tbilisi.

# Chapter 9

On Sunday morning, Rouben and I travelled westward to the Etchmiatzin cathedral – the headquarters of the Armenian Apostolic Church. It was one of the main pilgrimage places of Christianity for all Armenians. 'This is not just a monastery,' he said, 'but an entire complex of old and new churches with different architectures.'

'Like Geghard, you mean?' I asked.

'No, this is located in a very different setting; you'll see.'

Along the way, after a moment of silence, he tried to make conversation. 'Have you heard about the protocols between Armenia and Turkey to establish diplomatic ties, back in 2010?'

'I was told they've not been ratified. According to diaspora leaders, most of the protocols are in Turkey's favour and would disregard Armenian national aspirations,' I said.

'But the population in Armenia generally welcomed the normalization of relations between the two countries at the time,' Rouben replied.

'The diaspora also objects to another protocol clause,

which commits Armenia to recognizing its existing border with Turkey, for it would preclude future Armenian territorial claims to areas in Eastern Turkey that were populated by their ancestors until the 1915–18 massacres.'

'Turkey will never cede any land to us,' he said firmly.

'Even so, the Armenian claims should not be ignored. According to the diaspora, the president of Armenia made a big mistake by inviting his Turkish counterpart to attend a football match in Yerevan between the two countries' national teams, without official recognition of the Genocide.'

'I remember that, and he later came to regret his invitation to the Turkish president,' Rouben said.

'Oh, why?' I asked, surprised.

'Because the government of Turkey came up with absurd preconditions for the ratification of the protocols.'

We arrived at Etchmiatzin, which contained several early medieval churches in its complex. We walked past gardens, monuments and administrative church buildings. After a short while, the church bells tolled several times and we saw about 100 priests walking two-by-two in procession to the cathedral for Sunday Service.

'The church is the oldest pilgrimage site for all Armenians worldwide,' Rouben told me. 'It was built on the remains of a pagan temple in the early fourth century, by St Gregory, soon after Armenia's conversion to Christianity.'

'The Illuminator, you mean?'

'Yes,' Rouben replied, 'Gregory had a vision of Jesus appearing as a heroic figure of light, descending from Heaven. He struck the ground with a golden hammer, indicating the place where the cathedral was to be established, and named it "Etchmiatzin", meaning "the Only–Begotten has descended".'

We made our way into the small cathedral, its painted upper walls and ceilings leading to the interior of the stunning dome. In the presence of priests, monks and worshippers – the women veiled – Armenian chants, with a hymn to Jesus Christ, were sung with great solemnity. This was followed by the chanting of specific Bible passages by an ordained deacon during the Divine Liturgy (*"Patarak"* in Armenian). The worshippers then took communion and made a point of kissing the cross in the centre of the church.

After mass, we bought admission tickets and visited the small museum, in which there was a large collection of church relics; vestments, crowns, manuscripts, and a right-hand-shaped reliquary. Among the items on display was the spear with which Jesus was pierced on the cross. The lance was in a silver-gilt case with hinged doors. There was also a portion of Noah's Ark; a piece of reddish-coloured petrified wood about twelve inches by nine, and about an inch thick, which was kept in a golden casket.

On our way back to Yerevan, Rouben remembered, 'It is said that the portion of the Ark was brought down by one of the monastery's monks, St Jacob.'

'Did he climb Mount Ararat? I asked curiously.

Rouben nodded. 'On several occasions, he attempted a climb up the mountain but, exhausted by his efforts, he fell asleep. Tradition says that one day, during a deep sleep, an angel appeared in a dream and placed a fragment of the Ark on his chest as a reward for his faith.'

'Fascinating story. Mount Ararat and the Ark were just names for me in the past. Where do you think the starting point is for such an expedition?'

'From a town named Dogybayazt on the Turkish side of the mountain, now populated entirely by Kurds; some of them have Armenian blood, you know, but they've been converted to Islam, during and after the Armenian Genocide.'

Throughout the centuries, there had been many who had tried to pinpoint the location of Noah's Ark on Mount Ararat; including an Armenian bishop, British scientists, and American and Russian aviators or explorers. However, avalanches, violent storms, winds of a hundred miles an hour and below-zero temperatures made the climbing painful and often impossible for an expedition team. The glaciers sometimes dislodged and broke into segments, separated by thirty- to forty-metre-deep crevasses into which climbers often fell.

In spite of many dangers, every now and then an Ark-seeker reaped a reward for his efforts by uncovering a new piece of "data". One such case was of an Armenian, known only as Hagopian, who claimed to have seen the Ark in 1908 but his account seemed to contradict other statements. George Jefferson Green asserted that he spotted the Ark from a helicopter in 1953. He described it as being situated about two-thirds of the way up the peak, on a large rock shelf near a vertical cliff. Only one third of it was visible, the rest being submerged in snow and mud. At around the same level, James Frazier claimed to have seen the Ark, in a small lake and a dense swamp.

John Libi, an experienced mountain-climber, tried eight times in fifteen years to locate the Ark. During his first expedition in 1954, when he was chased by two huge bears near the ice cap, he found – 500 feet below the summit, locked in place by rock formations – three huge stone corrals and high walls that seemed to him to have been used to house animals. In 1967, extreme cold weather on Mount Ararat forced Libi and his group off the mountain and claimed the life of a climber.

Eryl Cummings, known as the dean of archaeologists, claimed to have uncovered an amazing amount of information concerning the existence of the Ark. He argued that if the super-structure of Noah's Ark was still extant on Mount Ararat, its remains should be found on the northwest to north-east quadrant of the mountain, as indicated by many reported sightings. From a picture taken by Cummings in 1966, experts found a mysterious object which had the shape of a long, slender barge with a walkway along the top, in a most inaccessible area which had a high cliff on one side. Unfortunately, overhanging clouds obscured much of the surrounding area in the picture, thus making it difficult to identify the location of the Ark.

Experts concluded that if the Ark did indeed remain on Mount Ararat, it must have been in an area where the glacier was stationary. A moving glacier could travel with tremendous force and a wooden structure like the Ark could not survive in its path. If the Ark was to be preserved, it would have to have been consistently frozen in a stable area, protected from these destructive forces.

# Chapter 10

The next day, at my request, Rouben and I went for a ride in his car through some of the villages in Armenia. I thought the visit would help me capture not only the daily life of the people there but also the mood and culture of the villages, which would be important for my understanding of those living in rural places. Many of the roads still remained in a dilapidated state; a driver had to focus hard to ensure the vehicle reached its destination without a puncture or breakdown.

I noticed there was a stark difference between life in Yerevan and anywhere else in the country. A fifteen-minute ride or stroll through any village was enough to uncover the disparity in privilege, wealth and experience. Although the pace of life was slow and easy, earnings demanded a lot of physical effort and patience. Since the Soviet factories had closed and jobs vanished, the middle-aged and the elderly were left behind by young migrant workers. Some families lived on a farm, others were selling their fresh crops – vegetables and fruits – to survive. No matter how difficult the villagers' living conditions were, they did not look either despairing or unhappy. They coped with the problems and family members always helped each other out.

At one place, a family with one child invited us for a coffee and we talked about village life, after which we had lunch, at their insistence. These people possessed a graciousness and warmth guaranteed to put their guests at ease.

At one point, the little boy darted towards his mother, who smiled at him and cuddled the kid, saying "I love you" in Armenian. I saw the child feeling most loved when he heard those words. I reflected on the loss of my own mother in the early years of immigration to the States. I had no recollection of it and only learned later that her name was Arpine. I believed that growing up without her and lacking this particular type of love in my life had been the crux of my own sense of deprivation. When they addressed their little enquiries to me about my parents I told them I had lost my mother when I was a child and a maid-servant took care of me while my father was at work. I saw tears welling up in the woman's eyes. Then our talk moved to my views about the homeland.

In another village, the atmosphere was one of disappointment and sadness. The women, who were left behind by their migrant husbands, called their village a "women's club", where they did everything from ploughing fields to raising children, and all else in between. During our brief encounter with one resident, she complained, 'It's hard to stay a woman in a village, and if only our country provided jobs, my husband wouldn't have left.'

A mother of five who, on her own, ploughed and sowed

fields and looked after cows and pigs when her husband left for Moscow each spring, sighed heavily, 'The whole burden of the household falls on my shoulders and the worst thing is that you never know if your husband will return or not.'

Nevertheless, they all accepted Armenia as their home, for better or for worse.

On our way back to Yerevan, I said to Rouben, 'There's something that we just don't have in diaspora. I often hear "*jan*" when people address each other here, what does it mean?'

Rouben laughed and explained, 'It's a term like "sweetheart" or "darling" that is attached to the end of someone's first name to express love.'

When we reached the city, he turned the car onto a big avenue. 'This is the Marshal Baghramian Avenue,' he said, 'home to a number of foreign embassies and government buildings.' He slowed down the car to show me something. 'Look there!' he pointed to the right side of the avenue, 'that's the presidential palace. Can you see the two statues within its grounds?'

I nodded my head in acknowledgment and he continued. 'The one on the right is of Noah and the other of Tigran the Great. You can admire the statues as you walk or drive. If you stop, you will be told to move on by the police guarding the palace.'

'Same law applies everywhere,' I said.

'Armenia was once an empire, during Tigran's reign, and it extended from the shores of the Caspian Sea to the Mediterranean. The popular expression used by Armenians is "Sea to Sea Armenia".'

The last words rang in my mind and I instantly recalled

the name of this warrior king through my history research back in Boston. 'The Armenian nation suffered a humiliating capitulation,' I said, 'and the divisions within their monarchy helped to overthrow the king.'

'We failed to present a united front against the enemy at the time,' Rouben agreed. 'Tigran's two sons were executed for their part in the plot to depose their father and his third young son, who rebelled against him, joined forces with Pompey and invaded his father's kingdom. Can you imagine that?'

I lowered my head. 'It's simply tragic,' I said.

'The Cilician kingdom had suffered a similar tragedy, you know. I think that was during the reign of the last Latin king, Leon V.'

'Armenians have caused more damage to their country than their enemies. History has shown that they were too politically illiterate to make serious political choices,' I said.

'And they failed to take a rational approach to their problems,' Rouben added.

He dropped me at the hotel and I thanked him for the great tour.

Tigran the Great reigned from 95 BC to 55 BC, during which time he occupied a great deal of land. No other Armenian ruler ever succeeded in surpassing the gains he had made. Greater Armenia reached its culmination of power during his reign, comprising a territory of 316,000 square kilometres, divided into fifteen provinces. According to legend, a weird obsession with waterfalls was the source of all Tigran's power and wisdom. Every time he was marching back with his army from foreign land into

Armenia, he would jump in the waterfalls and bathe for a long time. After that, he would return to his palace, well refreshed. Asked one day by one of his loyal servants about his need to visit the waterfall, the king answered by revealing a secret. 'I always bathe in the waterfalls so that the foreign dust upon me may be washed away and I may feel the spirit of my ancestors. The water in Armenia gives me strength and power for new battles ahead.'

Tigran was an ambitious, resourceful, and yet strangely erratic ruler. He was known for his magnificent silver coinage, which was the finest ever struck by an Armenian monarch. Despite his royal position, he was a wise and humble man, preferring to provide luxury to his own people. Tigran's capital, Tigranagert, had ambitions to become one of the centres of Hellenistic art, science and literature. Tigran fought wars against the Parthians and Seleucids, in what is today Syria, and later with the Roman army, with which his third son colluded. Rome, which could not allow another nation to grow strong enough to challenge its own power, marshalled its military strength and eventually reduced Armenia to its original geographical boundaries. In 66 BC, the old veteran monarch surrendered and accepted the hard terms of the Roman conqueror, who gave him back the remnants of his kingdom in return for a huge accolade. As for Tigran's rebellious son and heir, Pompey treated him coldly and took him back as a prisoner to Rome, where he was put to death.

After that, Tigran continued to reign in Artashat, Armenia's ancient capital, until his own death in 55 BC.

# Chapter 11

Since 189 BC, Nagorno Karabakh had been the tenth province of the kingdom of Armenia. This area of about 6500 square kilometres, generally considered as "the cradle of civilization", belonged to the five Armenian duchies and was governed by hereditary feudal lords who attempted to free themselves from foreign Muslim dominance – attacks by the Ottoman and Persian armies, and nomadic tribe invasions. After the collapse of the Russian empire, Karabakh became a theatre of war again and due to the wrong decision of Stalin in 1921, the disputed territory was given to Azerbaijan as an autonomous province. Its Armenian population of around 200,000 became subject to racial harassment and violence. However, with the Soviet Army firmly in control of the region, after several decades the conflict died down.

In February 1988, anti-Armenian pogroms in Baku and Soumgait, in which thousands of Armenians were cruelly killed, led to the fight for independence by the vast majority of the Karabakh Armenian population. During the dissolution of the Soviet Union, the struggle over the region's future re-emerged and further escalated into full-scale war, when both Azerbaijan and Armenia attained independence in late 1991.

Two years later, the conflict had caused thousands of casualties and left about 20,000 killed and 60,000 wounded, with close to a million refugees on both sides. On 12 May 1994, a ceasefire was reached through Russian negotiations. Backed by Armenia, the Karabakh Armenian forces, of which Vazgen Sargsyan was the military commander, had since controlled the region and a large area around it as part of a "security zone". This was widely regarded as a victory by Armenians.

Following twenty-two years of relative cease-fire between the breakaway Republic of Nagorno-Karabakh and Azerbaijan, large-scale military operations suddenly resumed along the line of contact, during the course of the four-day war in April 2016, which killed more than 100 Armenian soldiers and an unknown number of Azerbaijanis. Once again, Russian intervention ended the fighting. After that, cease-fire violations continued on a regular basis, with sporadic shootings creating more casualties on both sides. At this point, Azerbaijan was also shooting at villages in Armenia proper, and there was no meaningful Armenian response to this aggression. The continuation of these terrorist acts of Azerbaijan meant that whatever Armenia and Artsakh were doing was inadequate. This act of war by Azerbaijan against Armenia was being swept under the carpet without even a squeak from the so-called Collective Security Treaty Organization (CSTO), a group of supposed allies which included several Turkic states, managed by Russia.

The Organization for Security Cooperation in Europe

(OSCE) Minsk Group co-chair countries had established basic principles for the peaceful resolution of the Nagorno-Karabakh conflict. These principles were based on the Helsinki Final Act. Azerbaijan, however, wasn't cooperating with the OSCE Minsk Group peace process, arguing that the Armenian forces should withdraw from the disputed region.

On the other hand, the international community wasn't interested in resolving the Karabakh conflict swiftly, nor had it given a clear political assessment regarding Azerbaijan's continuous aggressions, preferring instead to appeal carefully to both sides. They asserted: "There is no military solution to the Nagorno-Karabakh conflict" and repeated that slogan from time to time.

I was watching the main evening news in my hotel room: 'An Armenian soldier has been killed in Nagorno-Karabakh in continuing cease-fire violations on the line of contact between Azerbaijani and Armenian troops. According to the Karabakh Defence Army, the 19-year-old conscript, Karen Ozounjian, was killed on Tuesday by sniper fire from Azerbaijani army positions north-east of Karabakh. An investigation is underway to clarify details of the incident.'

With more and more Armenian soldiers killed on the front line, I despaired of the young lives lost. Although they were understandably patriotic, fighting for a land that belonged to them, I thought there was no honour and dignity when it was a meaningless death; one that should have been avoided.

The next day, I raised the Karabakh issue with Rouben, on our return from a tour of other historical sites.

'You know, another Armenian soldier was killed on the front line yesterday,' I said.

'Yes, that was on the news last night,' he said sadly and then slapped one hand against the steering wheel. 'Those sons of bitches are all scammers and liars. They agree to cease-fire, then violate it, and then blame us for the violation.'

'It is said that the Karabakh Armenian army lost seven military positions in the four-day April war, is that true?' I asked.

'Yes, but most of them have been recaptured by the Armenian forces. It was a surprise attack against us in the first place.'

'It's a shame they hadn't foreseen it,' I said. 'Armenian losses raised questions about their military readiness.'

'You see, we want to avoid fighting a big war, and if it is forced upon us, our government will then unilaterally recognize the independence of Nagorno-Karabakh. But it is impossible to negotiate with delusional terrorists who believe these lands belong to them.'

I suddenly recalled, 'There was a political scandal involving the sale of inferior weapons to the Karabakh army during the brief war. It turned out that the procurements had served to fill the pockets of the high-ranking officers.'

Rouben shook his head in disgust. 'The Minister of Defence was immediately sacked. What worries the government most is the significant increase in Azerbaijan's military strength, and Armenians protested against Russian new arms sales to Baku.'

'Russia is pulling the strings in the region and continues to play a dirty double game, trying to use the recent escalation of violence to its advantage,' I suggested.

'I don't doubt that, for there are no real friends in politics, only interests,' Rouben commented.

'Absolutely.'

'With both sides building up their military forces, the situation is becoming more serious and dangerous, you know.'

'I feel it's only a matter of time before all hell breaks loose.'

Rouben pulled over abruptly and asked in amazement, 'Another war?'

'I hope not, but I don't see any way out of this old conflict, do you?

'I think the Minsk Group will find a peaceful solution to the conflict sooner or later,' he said.

'You don't understand,' I retorted, 'Western countries, including Russia, are not interested in solving it. Nor do they intend to recognize Karabakh as an independent state.'

'War is mankind's most tragic and stupid folly,' he said, shaking his head.

'That's right. Like Israel, Armenia and Karabakh are surrounded by enemies, so it's important to have an effective secret intelligence agency and advanced military weapons to protect your army and your country. I think Armenia can and should follow the Israeli model in the military sense.'

'Armenia has received sophisticated missiles from Moscow to boost its defence capabilities,' Rouben said. He restarted the car and we drove away.

Russia provided Armenia with Iskandar-M short-range ballistic missile systems to balance the volatile military situation in the Caucasus region and to ensure that none of the parties to the conflict would have military advantage. This system was designed to destroy small targets at a distance of around 300 miles and could be fitted with nuclear warheads. On the other hand, Israel had been supplying Azerbaijan with weapons and intelligence technologies; this was viewed as an additional threat by the Armenian authorities. The April war demonstrated that most of the casualties on the Armenian side were not caused by Russian-supplied weapons but by Israeli kamikaze drones. As a result of those drones, Armenia officially lost fourteen T-72s, and a bus carrying volunteers.

The main focus of the military concept of Armenia was close interaction with Russia, which was expressed not only in the supply of new weapons to Armenia, the training of Armenian military personnel in military universities in Russia and the diverse integration of the armed forces of Armenia and Russia, but also with direct military support in the case of aggravation of the Nagorno-Karabakh conflict. The Armenian government knew that Russia would not take a direct part in this fighting but Russian armed forces stationed in the 102nd military base of Gyumri – the second-largest city in Armenia – and Russian military aircraft stationed in Yerevan would cover Armenia directly in the event of any attack by the Azerbaijani army from its autonomous republic in the south.

# Chapter 12

When I started to interact with Armenians both in Boston and now in Yerevan, I realized how diverse they had become as an ethnographic entity. There was barely anything that pulled them all together. There existed a clear distinction between a French Armenian and an American Armenian; an Iraqi Armenian and a Cypriot Armenian; an Iranian Armenian and a Canadian Armenian; a Turkish Armenian and a British Armenian. In fact, over time, the diaspora Armenians adopted many of the characteristics of their host countries, but there was a lack of common ground between those different ethnic groups.

Armenia was a homogeneously populated country, Armenians making up 98% of the country's population. One reason for this was the Armenian language, which was practised at all educational institutions as the first language of the Republic of Armenia. Ethnic minorities comprised only two per cent of the population and included Russians, Ukrainians, Georgians, Kurds and Greeks. During my stay in the city, I was hearing mostly Eastern Armenian from the natives. Only a few instances of Western Armenian caught my ear and made me feel slightly more at ease.

Past historical events had dealt the Armenians a cruel blow and prevented them pursuing a common language and ideology, which could have paved the way for cultural, social and political unity. As a result, two segments of the Armenian people existed, practically isolated from each other. There was a considerable divide between the diaspora and homeland Armenians, on numerous issues. Each side thought that theirs was the true and only way.

Following Armenia's independence in 1991 and the Nagorno-Karabakh conflict, there had been a gradual shift in the first few years toward bridging the differences between the two sides and creating a positive environment in which they would work together. Starting with the diaspora's slow involvement in Armenia's economic development and the establishment of the Ministry of Diaspora of the Republic of Armenia in 2008, there had been some immigrations to the homeland from various parts of the world, including the repatriations of Syrian and Iraqi Armenian refugees. Meanwhile, the internet had played a significant role in re-establishing ties between the diaspora and the homeland.

During the Syrian civil war, many Syrian Armenians had been seeking refuge in Armenia. Most of them were descendants of victims of the Armenian Genocide. As the government did not have enough resources to help them, charitable organizations were stepping in and working with the Armenian authorities to build bridges between the government and the Syrian Armenian community. Accommodations were financed by diaspora Armenian communities.

From conversation with a local Armenian regarding those refugees, I gathered that some families came and left the country as they pleased; other people would get frustrated as they weren't able to find a job or pursue their careers. There were few people expressing the desire to come and live in their homeland. Of course, not everyone was coming with rose-tinted glasses. They were coming with a hope that the homeland would change their lives one day but also that they could use their experience or knowledge to change Armenia.

The village of Darbnik in the Ararat province had become home to twenty-eight families who escaped war in Iraq but had great difficulty adapting to the homeland. Locals always advised repatriates against settling here for good, saying they were taking a risk and that Armenia hadn't yet become the land of their dreams.

I learned from another local that immigration and emigration had always been part of the transient lives of Armenians. After World War II (1945–49), around 100,000 diaspora Armenians from all over the world resettled in the Soviet Republic of Armenia. The majority of the repatriates were the children and families of Armenians who had fled the Ottoman massacres. This event, which became known as the "Great Repatriation", was marred by factors such as socio-economic hardship, discrimination, and exile to labour camps in Siberia, never to return. Those unfortunate victims were targeted by Soviet intelligence agencies for real ties to Armenian nationalist organizations. It was a psychological and cultural shock. The repatriates had local Armenians looking at them suspiciously, ridiculing their habits and the way they talked the Western Armenian dialect. There was this demeaning term "*akhbar*", derived from "*yeghbayr*", the word for "brother" in Armenian, which was used by local Armenians in reference to their diaspora compatriots.

Having lived in such abysmal conditions, with no opportunity to leave the Soviet bloc or regain their confiscated citizenship papers, the newcomers warned their relatives abroad about any further move to Armenia by sending them cryptic messages or notes, very few of which reached their destinations due to the stringency of the censorship. It was many years before a great number of the repatriates left the "Sovietized" Armenia and returned to the diaspora communities in Europe, the United States and the Middle East.

From Soviet communism to Armenia's second independence, the recent years marked a turning point in the relations between the homeland and diaspora Armenians, with more openness about various issues. A new, promising shift was taking place, where cultural and social rifts were slowly closing in. Armenia was demonstrably immersed in supporting Western Armenian culture in the media, which had been a black-and-white issue in the past. Moreover, religious freedom, forced out of public and private life during the seventy years of Soviet rule, had been re-established in all parts of Armenia. However, most of the local Armenians who adhered to the Armenian Apostolic Church rarely attended church services. The creation of Birthright Armenia, which aimed to renew a sense of Armenian identity among diaspora youth and contribute to the country's development, won the praise of many Armenians worldwide. With these successive positive changes in the people and the country, the thick curtain which had divided the Armenian nation for a long time was pulled slightly back.

Perhaps it would take another generation or two to pull it entirely open.

# Chapter 13

Rouben drove me north-east, from Yerevan to Lake Sevan, along a lengthy highway. Set about 2000 metres above sea level - the highest-altitude lake in the world and the biggest in Caucasus – with its sandy beaches, Sevan is a popular holiday resort. In the past the lake's water level had dropped twenty metres but it had been rising again over recent years.

The Sevan monastery complex, which consisted of two churches, was located on top of the peninsula hill, along with the remains of an older church. We followed the trail that led up to the monastery. Old carved *khachkars* (cross stones) stood at the foot of the hill. We started our climb, pausing halfway up, the breeze blowing on our faces as we admired the entire lake before us, bare mountains in the background. It was as if our own world harmonized with the beauty of the lake's transparent, turquoise water; an incredible feeling of serenity.

As we were approaching the site, Rouben said, 'This monastery was once on the Sevan island, far away from people. Pumping water out of the lake caused the island to become a peninsula.'

'Oh, I see. When was the monastery built?' I asked.

'In 874 AD, by an Armenian princess, Mariam, the daughter of Ashot I, who later became a king. For several hundred years, it was a spiritual centre, housing many monks. One of the churches was dedicated to the Holy Apostles, the other to the Holy Mother of God.'

The monastery was built from crude black stone on the exterior. On the west side of the church was a quadrangular space, closed in on the other sides by three semi-circular apses. The interior had a beautiful old altar, used for services by the new seminary down the hill. We made our way out and I photographed the monastery then we sat on one of the benches in front of the churches.

'The lake's sparkling waters have given a home to many legends and famous stories,' Rouben said before he quoted Maxim Gorky, the Russian poet: "The waters of Sevan are like a piece of the sky that descended onto the earth and found its place in the mountains."'

We slowly descended the hill. 'Great place, so much history behind it,' I said.

As we strolled alongside the many fish restaurants and cafés on the shores of the lake, Rouben said, '*Ishkhan* fish is served here from twelve noon. "*Ishkhan*" means "fish-prince" in Armenian. It is caught in Lake Sevan. It's also a man's given name in Armenia. This freshwater fish has an excellent taste when it is well cooked.'

I glanced at my watch. It was half-past-twelve already. 'Okay, let's have that lunch,' I offered.

Surprised, Rouben smiled at me. 'I didn't mean to work up your appetite.'

'It's the fresh air that did that.'

We walked into the restaurant, where we were greeted by the waiter, who seated us at an empty table on the terrace. After a short while, he came back to take the order.

'One *Ishkhan* fish, please,' Rouben said.

'What would you like to drink?' the waiter asked gently. 'We have red and white wine and also beer.'

'I think beer will be fine,' I said, looking at Rouben, who agreed with a nod.

The waiter wrote down the order and passed it to the kitchen.

'You see, this *Ishkhan* fish cannot exist if the water is contaminated. What distinguishes the Armenian cuisine is its juicy and spicy taste, along with a variety of herbs,' Rouben said.

The waiter approached and put two plates and flatware on our table. He returned after ten minutes, carrying a tray loaded with the grilled fish, sauce, vegetables and drinks, which he placed on the table.

Rouben cut the fish in half and put one piece on my plate. 'It's quite delicious,' I said after tasting it, 'so soft that its flesh is falling off the bones.'

'Let me tell you a funny story,' he said. 'A father and son were out in their boat one day. While the father was fishing for trout, the boy suddenly became curious about fish and asked his father, "Do fish sleep with their eyes open?"

'The father replied, "Don't really know, son."

'A bit later, the boy looked at his father and asked, "Dad, how do fish breath underwater?"

'The father replied again, "Don't really know, son."

'The boy waited for a moment before he asked another question, "Do fish have feelings?"

'Once again the father replied, "Don't really know, son."

'Finally, the boy asked his father, "Dad, do you mind me asking you all of these questions?"

'"Of course not. If you don't ask questions, you'll never learn anything," replied the father.'

We laughed at the joke. Having settled the bill, we left the restaurant and headed back to the car. Half-completed hotels loomed behind smaller holiday-dwellings. On our way back to Yerevan, the journey was comfortable, with just the occasional cow herd passing through.

'You know, almost all the churches and monasteries were built on mountains or hilltops,' I said.

'That is something connected with the divine,' he said and went on, 'There's widespread belief among Christians over the centuries that the awe inspired by elevated locations helps to inspire thanksgiving.'

I saw some villagers standing on the side of the road, with large wooden boxes in front of them. 'What are those people doing there?' I asked.

'Selling fish,' he replied.

'Watch out!' I shouted as he swerved to avoid a stray goat.

'Shit! I could have killed the animal.'

After a short silence, I asked, 'What do the locals think of their current president?'

'He enjoys the support of only eight per cent of the population; he's widely mistrusted by the general public, calling for his resignation,' Rouben said.

'Presidents have always ignored such calls. But don't you think he should be praised for having built a new army and brought some democracy to the country?'

'Army, yes,' Rouben replied bluntly, 'but democracy? That's bullshit, it has not yet taken root here. What is important to our leader and his cronies is to amass wealth for themselves; the same goes for the country's mafia clans and corrupt officials who've always had close ties with the Russian mafia.'

'They must have their billions stashed away in foreign bank accounts,' I observed.

Rouben nodded in disgust. 'When ordinary people are struggling to make ends meet,' he added. 'Instinct tells me that there will be a real revolution in our country soon.'

'I was told that the president is a Karabakh native, is that true?' I asked.

'Yes,' he said, his voice full of disdain.

# Chapter 14

The next day, in the afternoon, Rouben and I rode to the oldest neighbourhood, "Kond", located on a hill in Yerevan – for me a new discovery. While we took a walking tour of the old district with narrow alleyways, I saw people living in the worst conditions in the absence of minimal accommodation – no water, gas or proper toilets. Dilapidated houses built on top of each other with cracks in the walls and crumbling ceilings posed a real risk to their occupants. It seemed to me these residents ignored everything and just went about their daily lives. I thought much history was behind the forgotten neighbourhood.

On our way back, Rouben pointed towards a sculpture in a memorial square in the city. 'That's the bust of Vazgen Sargsyan, he was the military commander of the Armenian forces in Nagorno-Karabakh,' he said.

'I've heard of him, a downtown street has his name,' I instantly recalled.

Rouben nodded and went on solemnly, 'Our history is full of tragedies and in our case we've also witnessed internal tragedies.'

'What do you mean?' I asked.

He grimaced as he pulled over. 'Vazgen was assassinated when he became Prime Minister later.'

'Can you tell me about it?'

He hesitated for a moment and then continued in a sombre tone, 'Back in 1999, five gunmen burst into the parliament chamber with machine guns and shot dead at close-range Vazgen and seven other top officials, injuring as many as twelve MPs in a matter of seconds – a disaster for the image of Armenia.'

I gaped at him in shock, 'But how did the gunmen manage to enter parliament with guns?'

'They were hidden under their overcoats; it was all prearranged with security men to let them pass.'

'Who were the perpetrators?' I asked.

'A young man by the name of Nairi Hunanian, his younger brother, and three other guys. The reason for this killing, as their leader stated, was "to overthrow the regime of bloodsuckers".'

'What happened then?'

'They held all the remaining MPs hostage and real negotiations began with the former president. To cut a long story short, the siege came to an end after the gunmen surrendered.'

I shook my head in disbelief while Rouben continued, 'People in Armenia couldn't have imagined that such an attack would happen. They were so shocked that they wondered if this could be real or just a nightmare.'

'What about the outcome of the investigation?'

He shrugged his shoulders. 'Nobody exactly knew who was behind this plot. It was believed to have been a *coup d'etat*. There were many allegations of foreign involvement at the time.'

'Even today, there are Western agents who want to weaken Armenia,' I said.

He nodded, 'Everything's possible in this evil world.'

While Rouben drove on, there was a moment of sombre silence in the car. 'This reminds me of another tragic event,' he added sadly.

'What's that?' I asked.

'Just a few months ago, in July, an armed opposition group of thirty men stormed a police building, killing one officer and holding more hostage...'

I interrupted Rouben as I recalled the event. 'I've heard of that; the stand-off came to an end when the gunmen surrendered.'

'We don't know if this group had any connection with the one, among them four women, arrested last year by the security service when they raided a house and found a big stockpile of weapons. It turned out that the group was involved in a conspiracy to assassinate political leaders and commit other terrorist acts in Armenia.'

'Today, terrorism seems not just more common, but more widespread,' I observed. 'As for the Armenians, they have experienced so much suffering at the hands of their enemies that it is unacceptable and a shame to shed today the blood of an Armenian by another Armenian.'

Rouben nodded solemnly as he pulled over at my hotel. He turned to me and said, 'Yeghishe Charents was a poet in Soviet Armenia and a victim of Stalin's purges in the 1930s. These are his words: "Oh, Armenian people, your only salvation lies in the power of your unity."'

'That's very true, the new generation of Armenians should learn a lesson from this,' I agreed.

On the way up to my hotel room, I felt a twinge of disappointment at the tragedies which were worrying developments for the future of Armenia.

# Chapter 15

Rouben took me in his car to Yerevan's railway station to show me a large patriotic monument. After parking the car, he guided me to the station's square, where the bronze statue of David of Sassoun stood on a stone pedestal. It depicted the epic Armenian hero on the back of a rearing horse, pulling out his huge sword, ready for a charge, his eyes full of fire.

'This is Yervand Kochar's work; the same sculptor of Vartan Mamikonian's monument, remember?'

I nodded and looked up at the imposing statue. 'It's amazing how the artist managed to have the horse stand on its rear legs,' I said.

'In fact, Kochar put lots of extra weight both on the back of the pedestal and the horse,' Rouben said and continued, 'David of Sassoun was incredibly patriotic, with a freedom-loving spirit. He drove Arab invaders out of Armenia and had a supernatural strength which came from the Spirit, and the regular use of butter and honey.'

'Where exactly is Sassoun?'

'It is a district in the Batman province of Turkey, that is

in historical Armenia.'

'And when does this legend take us back to?' I enquired.

'As a spoken tale, the poem itself dates back to the eighth century, but it wasn't written down before the 1870s. This epic, known as the *Daredevils of Sassoun*, is a long, heroic poem in four acts and tells about the adventures of four generations of a family, of which David is the third. There's this crucial battle when David challenges Melik, the ruler of the Arab caliphate of Musr, to a duel, and cuts him into two pieces.'

'What's the major theme of this epic poem?'

'It is that all heroes, including David, are fighting for justice, liberation of their homeland, and independence, to fulfil the aspirations and desires of the Armenian people.'

As we got back into the car, Rouben reminded me, 'Another legend, which is partially based on fact, tells us of Haik the Great, also known as Haik Nahabet, whose statue is erected in the Nork district. I'm going to take you there now.'

He started the car and drove to the north-east. When we arrived at our destination, a short climb led to the monument. A robust, curly-haired man wearing a lion skin, a quiver of arrows on his back, aimed his bow at the block of flats opposite.

'He's the forefather and founder of the first Armenian kingdom,' Rouben said.

'And when was that?' I asked.

'In the third Millennium before Christ. This mighty warrior-archer fought alongside Armens against the invading forces of the tyrant Bel of Babylon, in the land of Ararat. During the battle, Haik killed Bel with an arrow that flew with such a force it pierced Bel's armour and passed through his chest. Haik then had Bel's body hung from a big tree so that his family could see it.'

'He must be the most dominant figure in Armenia's national folklore,' I said.

'Absolutely,' Rouben replied. 'He lived more than a hundred years before his son, Armenak, succeeded him.'

'Is the major theme of this legend the same as the previous one, fighting for liberation of land and independence?'

'That's right.' Rouben continued after a pause, 'To become acquainted with a country, it's never enough to visit its places of interest; sometimes you simply need to pay attention to the monuments around you, which might give a more detailed picture of a particular nation.'

'I assume these monuments were designed and erected during the Soviet era.'

'Yes, within the period between 1920 and the 1980s.'

Like the epic stories of *Iliad* and *Odyssey*, the ancient tales of the Armenians were also filled with myths and legends, from which emerged a race of giants and epic heroes of stupendous stature. Tork, a descendant of Haik, had tremendous strength, breaking great stones with his hands and hurling huge rocks to sink the ships of his enemies.

Aram, whom the historian Moses of Khorene described as a great patriot, was a warrior who collected an army of 50,000 and drove the foreign invaders out of his fatherland. Epic poems praised Aram's valour in his conflicts with Barsham, King of Assyria, whom he eventually subdued.

He was succeeded by Ara the Handsome King, who had often been depicted as a model husband in Armenian literature. Semiramis, queen of Assyria and legendary wife of King Ninus, desired Ara to be her husband, promising him half of the kingdom, but he refused her offer, having a wife already. Eventually, the queen gave the order to capture the king alive and bring him to her but instead they brought his corpse. Semiramis mourned the deceased and tried every magic she could in a vain attempt to restore him to life.

Armenia developed cultural relations with neighbouring countries when it came under their influence; first of Persia, then of Greece and southern Assyria. Ancient Armenians were initially nature-worshippers who believed in luck, destiny and spirits. To them, even the flowers, trees, rivers and stones had spirits. Idols for deities had been introduced into Armenia before Hellenistic times. This faith in time was transformed to the worship of national gods.

Vahagn, the monster-slayer, identified with the Greek Heracles, was the god of fire and volcanoes, and also the god of courage, who conquered dragons. Astghik, identified with the Greek Aphrodite, was the goddess of love, beauty, and fertility. Aramazd, who corresponded to the Greek Zeus, was considered to be the principle god of Armenia; the creator of Heaven and Earth and the supreme legislator of justice. His daughter Anahit, identified with Artemis, was the goddess of motherhood. Mihr, regarded as the son of Aramazd, was also the god of sun, light and fire.

The Armenian pantheon, originally Urartian in nature, consisted both of native and imported gods and goddesses. As history refashioned them, only the notable ones later acquired a very specific Armenian character. During the fifth century BC, Armenians built temples in which there were statues of these gods and goddesses, to whom offerings were made at the altar where the gifts from the people were kept. When an Armenian king brought home captives, the images of their gods were placed in the temples beside those of the native gods.

The Armenians had their share of legends, in which gods, spirits, immortal superheroes and the forces of nature played dominant roles in their lives. There was no god of evil in the Armenian pantheon and their epic heroes were always described as fighting against evil spirits. In 53 AD, Zoroastrianism was spread in the Armenian highlands; probably during the Achaemenian and Parthian periods. This pre-Islamic, dualistic religion of Persia had a major influence on the Armenians and their mythology. It was a faith based on the highest moral standards and the source of such conceptions as good and evil, Heaven and Hell, last judgement, eternal afterlife, etc.; all of which were very similar to the Scriptures. Since then, Zoroastrian traditions were very much part of Armenian spiritual and material culture and were later absorbed into the Armenian Christian faith.

# Chapter 16

I pulled out my cell phone and called Rouben to find out what was on his schedule for the day. He said he would like to take me to the ancient Urartrian fortress of Erebuni, on the outskirts of the city. I instantly recalled the name Urartu from my research and told Rouben that I was really keen to see this archaeological site. Half an hour later, he picked me up from the hotel and we were on our way.

'This amazing site is also known as Arin Bert, meaning the "Fortress of Blood". The name Yerevan comes from the ancient name Erebuni, one of the oldest cities in the world. As you may know, it was founded twenty-nine years before Rome and it is about the same age as Babylon.'

'I've read something like that,' I recalled.

'There are of course different interpretations of the origin of Yerevan's name, which you can find out about on the internet. One of them refers to Noah and his Ark, which landed on Mount Ararat. As he came out of the Ark, after the flood waters had completely receded, Noah is believed to have looked in the direction of a land that is today Yerevan, and exclaimed "Yerevats!", meaning: "It appeared!"'

'That's interesting, you know. I will definitely do a web search for that,' I said.

Rouben drove on to a grand avenue, at the end of which I caught sight of the fortress surrounded by twelve-metre-high clay walls, atop a hill with a long stairway leading to the fort above. After parking the car, we walked past the Erebuni museum, in which a big collection of finds from the ancient fortress was displayed. We climbed the hill from its southern slope. As we walked, Rouben told me, 'Erebuni was founded in 782 BC by Argishti I, one of the most powerful kings of Urartu. The fortress, the first of its kind, was built as a military stronghold to protect the kingdom from northern invasions.'

'It's impressive that the remains of a 3000-year-old fortress have been preserved to this day,' I said.

The exterior walls of the fortress were erected in three rows. A six-column portico that stood at the entrance of the citadel was painted with colourful frescoes and the stairway leading up to it was flanked by bronze figures, of winged bulls with human heads. We stepped into the yard of the citadel, which was made of clay-coated adobe floors that were faced with stone slabs. 'Ceremonies held by the personal guards of the king and guards of the fortress garrison took place just here,' Rouben stretched his arms, indicating the place.

In the centre of the citadel was the palace, its inner walls adorned with beautiful mural paintings, depicting scenes of farming and hunting. From there, we made our way through a passage into the religious part of the fortress, where the temple to the god Khaldi was situated in the form of a pyramid tower, consisting of a number of storeys and presenting the appearance of a series of terraces. The hall, surrounded by two rows of twelve wooden columns, was decorated with multi-coloured wall paintings, depicting human figures, gods and floral designs. There was also an altar for sacrifices.

'We don't know for sure if this was part of the original Urartian palace, or just an addition made to become a Persian palace,' Rouben said and went on, 'However, some rooms have been rebuilt and painted to show how things would have looked back in those days.'

There were two temples at the heart of the palace and behind them a Zoroastrian-type fire temple. At either side of the entrance to the temple dedicated to the god Susi were inscriptions carved on the basalt walls, in cuneiform writing.

'Do you know what this inscription reads?' I asked with interest.

'I was just going to tell you,' Rouben said. 'It says: "Argishti, son of Menua, built this temple on a deserted land", that he's a great king of the land of Urartu and ruler of Tushpa, its capital.'

Further ahead, enormous jars made of fine clay stood in well-organized rows. 'These are used for storing food and wine,' Rouben said. 'Do you see the small markings on the side of these containers?'

I nodded.

'They indicate the amount that could be stored inside.'

There were also larger vessels, buried half-way into the soil. I admired them for a moment, wondering about the people who had once used them.

We came down the hill, heading back to Rouben's car. 'The fortress was the residence of King Argishti,' he said, 'who conquered many territories and expanded his kingdom beyond its traditional boundaries.'

During the reign of King Argishti, the city-fortresses of Erebuni (modern Yerevan) and Argishtikhinili (Armavir) were built; water channels were dug; and temples, palaces and barns were constructed. Agriculture, handicrafts and trade developed quite intensively. Moreover, the kingdom of Van reached the zenith of its military power. Argishti I continued his victorious northern invasions and conquered more lands in the basin of Lake Sevan. Fighting against Assyria, Argishti got the upper hand and pushed back Assyria's influence, beyond the borders of Northern Mesopotamia, the Commagene, and Northern Assyria. He took over the military and trade routes of the regions of Eastern Mesopotamia and the south-east of Asia Minor, and united the whole Armenian Highlands.

Later, the kings who succeeded Argishti turned Erebuni into their residence during their military campaigns against Northern invaders. Ultimately, Urartu, after its conquests, and rivalling for more than two centuries the claims of Assyria, fell in 585 BC, before the might of the Median and Achaemenid empires. Despite countless invasions, Erebuni was never abandoned, having an excellent position strategically and thus, being always inhabited by native Armenians, it eventually became the city of Yerevan.

I did some research into Yerevan's etymology and found out that the first interpretation of the city name was related to the name of the founder of the city, Argishti I, who was thought to be King Ara I. The city was named "Aravan" after him, meaning the city of Ara, considering the fact that

Armenian kings had always named cities after them. Those kings, including Ara, were given the nicknames "Eri" or "Ere" and eventually the city's name became known as "Erevan" or "Erivan". The second interpretation referred to the Armenian king, Yervand IV, who was the last leader of the Orontid Dynasty, and founder of the city of Yervandashat. The third interpretation suggested that when Yerevan was under Turkish, and later Persian, rule, the city was known in Persian as "Iravan".

Further research showed the city was called Yerevan from the seventh century, when it was captured by Arab, and later Seljuk, Turks and served as a crossroad for caravan routes between Europe and India. During the ninth and eleventh centuries, Yerevan was part of the Bagratuni Armenian Kingdom. In the late fourteenth century, the city was taken and pillaged by Tamerlane, also known as Timur and Tamburlaine; a brutal leader of Turkish descent, who dreamed about world domination and whose expanding empire stretched from Delhi to Anatolia (Asia Minor).

Both Persians and Ottomans endlessly fought for domination of Yerevan and its strategic significance. When the second Russo-Persian war broke out, lasting from 1826 to 1828, the city was liberated by Russian forces. Supported by Tsarist Russia, the Armenian resettlements from Persia and Turkey resulted in the increase of the Armenian population in Yerevan, which was finally given a city status in 1850, with the establishment of a number of institutions, colleges and factories.

# Chapter 17

Rouben took me to the Yervand Kochar museum, on the Mesrop Mashtots Avenue. Kochar was a prominent Armenian painter and sculptor, whose work had been exhibited in Paris in the 1920s, alongside work by Pablo Picasso, Georges Braque, and other avant-garde masters. The museum showcased various works created throughout Kochar's career, with labels in English. The top and middle floors of the three-storey building exhibited paintings and sculptures from 1898–1970. Kochar was the founder of "Painting in Space" – an innovative expression of the relationship between time and space through the use of various materials and art forms. One of the colourful paintings depicted the disaster of war. We strolled around the hall and paused before the beautiful illustrations of the epic *Daredevils of Sassoun*.

'These works are by the same artist who erected the statue of David of Sassoun. I told you about this folk epic dealing with the adventures of David, remember?' Rouben said.

'Of course I do.'

Among the artist's works were David with Kurkik Jalali, David's fight with Msra Melik, Mher wrestling with a lion, and finally Tigran the Great and Vartan Mamikonian. After a time, we descended to the ground floor, which displayed the artist's drawings.

Back in the car, Rouben said, 'Kochar was imprisoned on politically motivated charges in the 1940s but he was released later.' After a short while he asked, 'Today's Saturday, isn't it?'

'It is indeed,' I said.

'On the last Saturday of each month,' he went on, 'entrance to the State History Museum is free. I promised I would take you there one day, remember?'

'Yes, that would be great.'

He turned onto a street called Apovian, which led to the Republic Square. Parking the car down the street, we got out and headed towards the museum. Inside the building, we took the elevator to the top floor, planning to start there and work our way down to the first. The collection of Armenian art was displayed in the gallery halls and highlighted the history of national fine art and decorative-applied art. Museum workers were watching visitors, trying to make sure nobody was taking photos inside. Rouben acquainted me with prominent painters like Surenyants, whose paintings depicted scenes from fairy tales and historical events. Next came Hovnatanyan, one of the last generation of painters, who was a portrait artist – princes, the wealthy and the clergy became the main subjects of his work.

Rouben pointed to a portrait of a woman and said, 'This is known as the Armenian *Mona Lisa*.'

We roamed around the next gallery, which contained the

works of Ivan Aivazovsky. I examined his paintings of landscapes and seascapes. 'Aivazovsky was a great Russian painter of Armenian descent. He contributed over 6000 paintings to the art world,' Rouben said and nodded towards one of the paintings. 'Look, how the water shimmers against the full moon.'

As we paused at another painting, Rouben went on, 'See how the sky is filled with light and how the orange glow of the sun gleams through the clouds?'

'Great work,' I said.

Other pieces by the artist depicted marine landscapes and battle scenes.

*The Chesmensky Fight*, oil on canvas, was one of his masterpieces. After closely examining it I said, 'It's amazing how the artist conveyed the horror of the battle in his painting.'

We descended to the lower floors, where an important archaeological collection of Armenia's culture was displayed, from the Stone Age through to the mediaeval period, along with ancient objects of eastern regional countries; the Byzantine empire and Assyria. In the first department there were bronze statuettes, painted ceramics, arms and weapons with sculptural ornamentation and specimens of gold from the Armenian state of Urartu.

'Most of the items in this hall are not labelled in English. Visitors should understand what they're going to see,' I remarked.

'You're right. Unless you're fluent in Armenian, you're out of luck,' said Rouben.

'Doesn't the museum provide multi-language brochures?'

Rouben shook his head.

Further ahead, we stopped to look at an artefact dating back to the Copper Age – the world's oldest leather shoe. The 5500-year-old oval-shaped shoe, about nine-and-a-half inches long and three inches wide, was made from a single piece of cowhide, stuffed with dry grass, and laced along the seams at the front and back with a leather cord.

'This shoe was found about a decade ago, in a cave in southern Armenia, on the border with Iran and Turkey,' Rouben said.

I examined the shoe, agape. 'It is stunningly preserved.'

'According to specialists, the dry and cool conditions inside the cave, as well as the layer of sheep dung above the shoe, helped to protect it against decay.'

'I wonder if it belonged to a man or a woman.'

'That is not known,' he replied.

We walked past wooden carts and chariots from the fifteenth and fourteenth centuries BC.

There was a huge collection of various gold, silver, and copper coins from the Seleucid, Parthian, Byzantine, and Roman eras, along with coins of the Armenian Artaxiad dynasty (189 BC–6 AD) and the Armenian kingdom of Cilicia (1080–1375 AD).

When I returned to my hotel, I had much to think about. The history of Armenia was rich and strong but politically it felt unsettled, even now.

# Chapter 18

Armenia had no choice in its foreign policy but to develop a strategic alliance with Russia as the former lacked sufficient resources to counter both Azerbaijan and Turkey militarily. For Russia, Armenia had a huge geopolitical value, being a foothold in the south Caucasus, which it used to keep the entire region in check. The legally binding guarantees provided by Russia, through bilateral agreement and in multilateral format, were indispensable for Armenia. No other country in the region or abroad was willing or able to provide the necessary security guarantees.

History was another factor that influenced Armenia's attitude towards Russia. Since the beginning of the eighteenth century, Russia had been perceived in Armenian political and religious circles as the only state capable of liberating Armenia from Persian and Ottoman domination. The perception of Russia as a "saviour" became popular among Armenians in the early nineteenth century, after Russia's victory over the Persians and the incorporation of Eastern Armenia into the Russian empire. Even the 1920–21 Russia-Turkey alliance had not substantially damaged the image of Russia among Armenian society. Soviet propaganda at the time reinforced the view that Russia was Armenia's saviour and "big brother", without whose support Armenians would be in danger of total annihilation.

While Armenia had always had a special relationship with Russia, and hosted Russian troops on its territory, the government also worked to cultivate a good relationship with the United States and the European Union. Armenia was in desperate need of the multifaceted assistance offered by Western institutions. Armenian society on the whole viewed the reforms and modernization as the only viable option to guarantee development and statehood. However, Armenia was cautious not to anger Russia in its relations with the West, especially as Russia considered Western involvement in the post-Soviet space hostile actions.

In September 2013, Armenia decided to join the Russia-led Customs Union and Eurasian Economic Union. This move effectively voided the signature of the Association Agreement with the EU, which had been negotiated earlier. In December 2015, Armenia launched new negotiations with the EU, in an effort to keep its foreign policy balanced. In the meantime, US-Armenia relations were developing positively, in some cases due to the active involvement of Armenian lobbyists in the US.

On the other hand, the current strategic rift between Russia and the US complicated Armenian efforts to pursue this balanced policy. The Western rhetoric on containment against Russia could eventually put Armenia under tougher Russian pressure to restrict its interactions with the US and NATO. The relations of the Republic of Armenia with Western countries and structures were built in rather ambiguous geopolitical conditions. It was not a secret that

Armenia had clearly tilted toward the pro-Russian vector, and that its entire political, defence and economic security doctrine was integrated into pro-Russian structures such as the CSTO.

One of the most important elements of the complementary policy of official Yerevan was the progressive cooperation with the NATO bloc. Armenian servicemen took an active part in peacekeeping operations under the auspices of NATO in Afghanistan and Kosovo. Armenia refused to participate in NATO exercises, partly as a result of the pressure from the Russian side, considering the growing tensions between Russia and the United States, and also due to some political jealousy towards countries that had better relationships with Western political and military structures.

But the main reason for Armenia's refusal to participate in the NATO exercises was the whole complexity of problems facing the Armenian leadership, the most important of which was the issue of ensuring the security of Armenia and Artsakh in a probable military confrontation with Azerbaijan. Thus, Armenian foreign policy would have to deal with the hard task of keeping its partnership with the West whilst simultaneously avoiding its strategic alliance with Moscow being jeopardised.

# Chapter 19

On a part-cloudy, part-sunny day, Rouben and I set off for the Amberd Fortress, which was located on the southern slopes of Mount Aragats, some fifty kilometres north-west from Yerevan. In the suburbs, we saw a young bearded man with a backpack; thumb up, hitchhiking, on the roadside ahead.

'He looks like a foreigner to me,' I said.

'Yeah, not many locals hitch a lift in Armenia. Would you like me to pick him up?'

I shrugged, 'I don't know.'

'We'd better not, it's sometimes dangerous to give a ride to a stranger,' he said and accelerated.

After half an hour's drive, we branched off into the rural area of the country. Rouben turned the car radio on and Armenian traditional music came through the speakers.

'What kind of instrument are we listening to?' I asked.

'*Duduk*,' he said, 'it is one of the most popular Armenian music instruments. Do you like it?'

'Yes, it has a warm, soft sound.'

Rouben pointed across the landscape towards what

looked like a high mountain with four peaks. 'That's Mount Aragats, which became a permanent home for mountaineers. The mountaintop has several hidden pagan and early Christian shrines.'

When we reached the village of Byurakan fifteen minutes later, Rouben pointed to a distant building. 'Look there,' he said, 'that's the observatory; one of the main astronomy centres of the former Soviet Union. It was founded by the prominent scientist Victor Ambartsumian.'

Outside the village, the area was virtually uninhabited. We passed through gently sloping hills on a serpentine road; the only humans being an occasional shepherd or beekeeper. There were many wild flowers all around. The fortress came into view as we turned a corner. It stood on a rocky cliff; a witness to centuries of turbulent history.

I looked at the imposing site, agape. 'Wow, that's a big fortress!'

'Yeah, you know, it is quite impossible to get here in winter, when everything is covered in snow,' Rouben said.

'Of course, the road would be closed,' I said. 'What does "Amberd" mean?'

'A fortress in the clouds; given its elevation at 2200 metres.'

Rouben left the car down the road and we slowly climbed the hill towards the fortress, which was protected on two sides with deep gorges at the junction of two rivers. There was a small church slightly down the hill, in almost its original state.

'This seventh century fortress was built as a major strategic point for Armenian family rulers who made it their residence,' Rouben explained. 'Despite its impregnable position, it was invaded by Seljuk Turks at the end of the eleventh century and later by Mongols, who captured and burned the castle, but it was reconstructed to serve as an outpost for many years.'

The thick walls of the fortress were made from massive, hewn basalt stones; presumably protection from shells. After paying the entrance fee, we made our way into the princely castle; a three-storey structure fitted with a majestic staircase and protected by walls with inclined towers which were still partially standing. I could see on each floor only a rudimentary outline of the layout of the rooms.

'The inside of the castle must have been sumptuous at one time,' I observed.

'Oh, yes, fragments uncovered during excavation showed rooms decorated with elegant carvings and the walls were ornamented with silk, gold and silver.'

Outside the palace were the ruins of a bathhouse decorated with frescoes; also parts of a secret passage, which attracted my attention.

'What's that hole over there?' I asked with interest.

'During excavations, many underground walkways leading to rivers were found; there used to be a water-supply system for the bath,' Rouben explained.

We also visited the neighbouring church, which bore an inscription above the entry, indicating that it was built in 1026 by Prince Vahram Pahlavouni. With a cruciform interior and a rectangular exterior, the church was simple and crowned by an umbrella-shaped dome. We walked around the fort complex and enjoyed the amazing views of the canyons and landscape – a very peaceful and remote place in a rough, mountainous region.

On our way back to the car I said, 'The fort seems to be

well preserved, you know.'

'Yes, a large part of the fortification walls remains intact; only a small section collapsed in recent years, and the structure urgently needed restoration.'

'I wonder what life in the castle was like?'

'In those times, life was not very easy. One problem was that the heating supplied only the royal family owners, while the soldiers and ordinary people had to somehow withstand the cold winters. During the day, servants prepared meals and men were busy with hunting. After breakfast, the lord and his family entered the church for morning service.'

'Was the Armenian Church involved in political affairs at the time?' I asked.

'Yes, because there was no statehood.'

'In my view, the church should be separate from the state and not interfere in political affairs.'

'That's the case in Armenia today,' Rouben affirmed.

# Chapter 20

The following day, Rouben and I drove westward to the Sardarabat Memorial, which was built in memory of the heroes who fell at the battle of Sardarabat against the Turks in 1918. Aware of the historical event, I didn't want to miss this site. Halfway to Sardarabat, Rouben pointed to the right, towards another structure, which was erected on a small hill and made of red tufa stone. 'That's the Musa Ler Memorial, dedicated to the heroic battles of self-defence and fallen heroes during the 1915 Armenian Genocide.'

Rouben recounted briefly the history of the monument and I gathered that Musa Ler, meaning "Moses mountain", was situated on the Eastern Mediterranean coast in what is today the Turkish province of Hatay. There were six Armenian villages on the slope of the small mountain. Most of the people living there, about 6000 in all, who ignored the deportation order, climbed up with supplies to the top of the mountain, where 300 combatants organized a resistance and for fifty-three days repelled continuous attacks by Turkish armed troops. Eventually, British and French naval ships came to the rescue and evacuated the remaining people to Port Said in Egypt.

As Rouben drove on he said, 'At the back of the Musa monument, there are two museums. One holds many documents related to the battle and the second represents traditions of Musalerians. Every year in September, people gather around the monument to celebrate the anniversary of the victory.'

'But it wasn't really a victory, was it?' I said. 'Although the Armenians fought bravely to defend their land, they were forced to leave it in the end.'

'But some of them returned when the area was under French mandate. In 1933, Franz Werfel, an Austrian Jew, published a historical novel, entitled *The Forty Days of Musa Dagh*. It first appeared in German, followed by the English version a year later, and since then it's been translated into various languages, including Turkish.'

After a short while, we arrived in Sardarabat. The complex extended over some fifty acres of parkland, through which a long pathway followed by a series of flights of steps led to the entrance of the memorial. On our way there, Rouben stopped for a minute and, pointing his index finger to the ground, said, 'This is the place where the course of history was changed. A makeshift army of poorly-armed, determined Armenians won a decisive victory over Turkish invaders in 1918 and saved what was left of Armenia. There would be no Armenia today without this terrific military success, thanks to the national hero, Aram Manukian.'

'Armenians have always been known to be brave and courageous fighters,' I said.

'They rarely were known for their aggression and always acted in self-defence. We're a peaceful nation unless we're forced to fight.'

We headed towards a wide square, flanked on two sides by two huge winged bulls of red tufa stone, symbolizing the victory of the people. We climbed a flight of stairs leading to the square, where a twenty-five-metre-high belfry rose up, with two rows of twelve bells hung at the top. As we paused and looked up at the monument, Rouben told me, 'These bells reflect a crucial moment in the country; a call to arms to prepare for the upcoming battle. Catholicos Kevork V ordered all church bells in Armenia to ring day and night in the days of the three battles of Sardarabad, Gharakilise, and Pash Abaran.'

We moved further ahead. A 180-foot-long curved wall, with one central arch, was flanked by a series of statues of eagles. 'The eagles represent the spirit of the fearless fighting men,' Rouben said.

Passing through the victory wall, on which were sculpted images of the battle, Rouben went on, 'Every year on 28 May, the locals and diaspora Armenians celebrate here the short-lived independence of the first Armenian republic, which laid the foundation of the third republic. These remained taboo issues in Soviet Armenia until the national awakening of the 1960s. After that, the construction of the monument dedicated to the battle began.'

'But Armenia is now facing the same problems and challenges it had 100 years ago, when it comes to next-door neighbours,' I said.

'Yes, unfortunately.'

To the left, five minutes' walk from the second memorial, was an ethnographic museum which exhibited historical and cultural objects from Armenia's heritage. We made our way into the building. I looked around. 'Looks like a fortress, with no windows.'

'Perhaps they want to protect the artefacts collection from sunlight damage,' Rouben replied.

The ground floor had galleries, in which numerous items of the battle, of ancient and medieval arts, and various traditional handicrafts, were on display. On the second floor, we studied objects ranging from ethnographic instruments, carpets and embroidery to national costumes, modern Armenian decorative ceramics and jewellery. As we came down and out of the museum, I said, 'There were some fascinating exhibits there.'

'You know, museums can be sometimes boring for foreign visitors. For them, the most attractive parts are the objects and paintings,' Rouben said.

'You know better than me; it's your job, but in my opinion, museums can and should be both entertaining and educational.'

On our way back to Yerevan, Rouben said, 'The architect of the memorials was Rafael Israelyan, who built numerous monuments in towns and villages.'

'Pretty good work,' I said. 'You know, all these monuments might not speak of anything to foreigners, but they do mean much for all Armenians.'

When we arrived in the city, Rouben pulled over at a semi-destroyed building. 'That's what is left of the home of Aram Manukian. He was one of the founders of the First Republic of Armenia and a member of the Armenian Revolutionary Federation. The commemorative plaque on the wall states that he once lived there.'

What I examined was just a façade in skeleton form, the wall blackened by decades of soot and substantial decay. 'An important historic site that remains part of old

Yerevan,' I said. 'But it's a shame that it has been left like that.'

'The government wants to restore the building and perhaps make it a museum.'

I photographed the building's façade before Rouben started the car and drove off. 'This street was renamed in his honour after our second independence,' he reminded me with a smile.

# Chapter 21

On my second Sunday in Armenia, I was sitting on a bench close to the fountains at the Republic Square, looking at the map of Armenia. It was unusually calm; almost warm. Since my arrival in Yerevan, I had kept a diary of my guided tour of each archaeological site and cultural monument I'd visited, using the internet when there was a requirement for further research on related topics. It was astonishing how many attractions, most of them difficult to reach, were packed within such a small territory – from the great view of snow-covered Mount Ararat, through the amazing canyons and gorges, to the mountaintop ancient fortresses and mystical monastery complexes carved into the walls of the cliffs. I reflected on how those historic sites, together with the modern capital city, typified the harmonious fusion of past and present.

After a short while, my mobile phone rang in my pocket. I pulled it out and it was Rouben, who told me he had got tickets for a performance of the *Gayane* ballet at 7.30 in the evening and he would pick me up from the hotel half an hour beforehand. I agreed; it was a good idea for something different. Hardly had I put my mobile phone back into my pocket when I heard a man's voice behind me, 'Excuse me.'

I turned round and saw a pitiful middle-aged man in shabby clothes. 'Are you a diaspora Armenian?' he asked.

I asked myself how he knew I was an Armenian from diaspora but quickly realized that I had been speaking the Western Armenian dialect with Rouben during our phone call.

'Yes,' I replied.

'My name's Ashot. May I ask where do you come from?'

'Boston.'

'Is there any corruption there?' he asked.

'Not to my knowledge,' I said.

He looked at me, disappointed, 'Well, there's a lot of it here, especially in the government. Our political leaders and their oligarch cronies are running the country with absolute selfishness, at the expense of its citizens. Oh, there's no justice in Armenia.'

I nodded in agreement.

'They never learn how to say enough is enough,' he continued, slightly angrily. 'You see, in this country it's impossible to become rich legitimately so there are those small sharks feeding on individuals' money, and also those big sharks feeding on public money.'

'Unfortunately, people in this century are more materialistic than ever before,' I said.

'You see, sir, we're living in a raw, troubled world where human greed and passion rule these days.' He allowed himself a small smile and waved goodbye to me. 'Have a nice day,' he said and walked away.

I thought the man's comments were entirely truthful and

I could see the sincerity in his eyes while he poured out his heart to me. On my way back to the hotel, which was only a few blocks from the Republic Square, I saw an accordionist standing on the pavement, playing an Armenian love song. There was a cup near to him with a few coins in it. I was about to walk past a beggar dressed in rags, with wrinkles on his face, when the desperate pleading in his voice just made me stop. 'Please,' he mumbled.

I looked at him while he continued to hold my gaze. 'Please,' he begged again.

I didn't think it was all part of the "get money" game, for the sadness in his eyes was just too real. I immediately started to feel bad, as if he was a relative of mine or someone I knew well. I pulled out my wallet and handed the guy a 5000-dram note; about ten US dollars. I saw the man's gloomy face brighten into a smile. Perhaps the poor guy had never received such an amount before, for he was so grateful and kept saying, "God bless you." Further ahead, another man was standing near a photo shop, his back against the wall - eyes focused on nothing – his right hand rattling a tin cup with a small coin in it.

On the opposite side of the pavement, an old woman with her medical documents in her hands, lost in her own world, was sitting on a stool next to a man who was selling flowers. As I approached the woman, the flower-seller told me she was collecting money to cure her diseases and that she had once had a higher education but fate had played a dirty game with her. I gave her a 5000-dram note also and she looked up at me, smiling her thanks. As I walked away, I noted that unlike in some other Asian countries, these Armenian street beggars were not harassing people and chasing after them for money.

Back in the hotel, I reflected on the day's events. I gathered that Yerevan was a cosmopolitan city, where greed and need co-mingled smoothly. The rich man, who owned the most expensive car in the world, enjoyed the wealth that he had while the poor beggar, who stood on the back street corner with a palm up all day long, asked for a few coins to prevent starvation. Ashot's words: "There's no justice in Armenia" rang twice in my mind. I had learned from a local Armenian that about half of the population lived below the poverty line – an astounding figure. Most of those affected by poverty either resided in rural areas along the nation's border or in isolated mountain villages, in old makeshift houses haphazardly mended with metal sheets or planks of wood. As for the families in extreme poverty, they relied on items they picked from the garbage in their neighbourhood; food, clothes, worn-out shoes, old tableware and fuel.

According to the Armenian National Statistics, more than 200 people committed suicide - mostly in the big cities - in January 2016, either by hanging themselves with a rope in their own apartments or jumping off a bridge or high building. Some observers linked the spike in the suicide rate to Armenia's hard economic condition – joblessness, debts and loss of hope. Others pointed to societal factors, such as social isolation or loneliness, severe depression and psychosis. Many others blamed the media for depicting "suicide" on TV as a normal way of problem-solving. There were reports of suicide even in Armenia's conscript army as a result of physical abuse and/or traumatic experiences. An increasing number of people under the age of forty-five were taking their own lives. Unfortunately, there had been no programmes provided by the Health Ministry to address the problem of the drastic rise in the suicide rate.

# Chapter 22

Rouben picked me up at 7.00 p.m. as agreed and drove directly to the Opera House.

'How was your day?' he asked.

'Fine, I guess. Those beggars on Amiryan Street are a pitiful sight,' I said.

'I personally don't give to beggars; only sometimes to real handicaps,' he said firmly.

Rouben drove into the opera's underground parking lot and left the car there. We climbed some flights of stairs to the square and headed, along with many fans of ballet, towards the grand opera building, which was illuminated at night. In front of the main entrance, on the north side of the building, was a statue. I was wondering who it represented. Rouben paused and said, 'This is Aram Khachaturian, the most renowned Soviet Armenian composer of the twentieth century. Have you heard his music?'

'Not yet,' I said.

'Pity, he's best known for his ballet music of *Gayane* and *Spartacus*.'

After entering the opera house, we headed towards the

concert hall, which was full of audience members. The interior of the auditorium was adorned with bas-reliefs and Armenian ornaments. On the way to finding our seats, an usher handed each of us a programme; a printed leaflet outlining the story of the *Gayane* ballet. As we took our seats, Rouben glanced at his watch. 'We've got ten minutes until the performance.'

In the programme, along with a brief synopsis of the plot, was a list of names of the principals. It said the ballet was based on an earlier ballet, composed in 1939 by Khachaturian, called *Happiness*. He started composing the score of *Gayane* in autumn 1941 and the ballet was first presented on 3 December 1942, on the small stage of the Perm State Theatre. The ballet, in four acts, conveyed the atmosphere of World War II and raised issues of patriotic convictions and treason. In later years, the plot was modified a couple of times to include elements of inter-ethnic love, betrayal and friendship.

The setting for the ballet is a co-operative cotton farm in Armenia, where Gayane, the heroine, is married to a drunk layabout named Giko, who always mistreats her. Gayane denounces her husband and Kazakov, the Soviet guard, eventually arrests Giko and three smugglers for conspiracy. Gayane ends her marriage with the drunkard and marries Kazakov. Their wedding provides the happy ending with the *Sabre Dance*.

Tonight, the Armenian Philharmonic Orchestra would be performing the ballet music, conducted by Eduard Topjan.

The auditorium lights gradually dimmed and the curtain rose to reveal a collective farm where Gayane's family – her father Ovanes, her brother Armen and younger sister Nune – are busy reaping cotton. They are all hard-working people, unlike Giko. She reprimands him for his misconduct and this escalates into quarrel. Kazakov arrives with a dance of welcome. When Giko sees Gayane presenting a bouquet to Kazakov, he snatches it from her and disappears. Act I quietly closes.

After a short while, Act II opens on the inside of Gayane's house. Friends are consoling Gayane, who is deploring Giko's misconduct. The singing voices of carpet-weavers can be heard in the background. As Giko returns, everyone goes out. While Gayane sings their child Ripsime to sleep, three smugglers appear on stage and see Giko, with whom they conspire, planning to share the public money they have misappropriated, to set fire to the cotton warehouse and flee abroad. Gayane overhears the conspiracy and admonishes her husband, who thrusts her into a room and locks her up.

After that, the act closes with a fifteen-minute interval.

The auditorium lights were turned on high and some audience members left their seats momentarily while others reviewed the rest of the programme. Rouben turned to me, 'What do you think of the performance so far?'

'Good,' I said.

'The composer has included Armenian and Caucasian tunes in his work, combined with classical and folk dances,' he said.

'Yes, wonderful duets,' I said. 'It's beautiful how all the parts interact with each other.'

'Wait until you see the end of the performance,' Rouben smiled at me.

The auditorium lights gradually dimmed. Complete silence swirled through the hall.

Act III opens on a Kurd's settlement near to the collective

farm. Among the people gathered there are Gayane's brother Armen and a Kurdish girl with her companion, Ismail. Giko and the three smugglers appear. Armen wonders what they are after and sends some Kurdish youths to fetch Kazakov. Having noticed this, Giko and his gang try to kill Armen, but Kazakov arrives just in time and arrests the three smugglers. Giko escapes and sets fire to the cotton warehouse. Trying to flee the scene, he is found by Gayane, who has managed to break out of the room in which she was imprisoned. Giko threatens that he will drop their child from a cliff. When Gayane refuses to yield, her husband stabs her with a dagger. Kazakov hears her screaming and, rushing in, he arrests Giko. The Soviet guard strives to calm Gayane's fears and as she recovers they fall in love with each other. Act III quietly closes.

After a short while, Act IV opens on a ceremony which is dedicated a year later to the reconstructed warehouse and the wedding of the couple – Kazakov and Gayane. The guest dancers brandish their sabres and perform the *Sabre Dance* – a fast tempo, repetitive theme with a pulsating rhythm; rich orchestrations including woodwind, brass, timpani, xylophone, and trombone instruments, the latter playing a series of *glissandos*. The second repetition of the theme is interrupted by a cymbal crash and the third is played in a higher chord. Then the coda descends and rises to the final note; a simple melody that expresses happiness and patriotism. Finally, the ballet ends with all the people's blessing for the wedding of the couple.

The performance drew enthusiastic applause as the auditorium lights were turned on. All the dancers reappeared on stage, after which a bouquet was brought in and handed to the heroine, who bowed in a gesture of deep appreciation. The audience continued to cheer and applaud until the curtain came down.

As we made our way out, alongside the other members of the audience, Rouben asked, smiling, 'Your views about the performance?'

'It was pretty good on the whole; I liked the *Sabre Dance* particularly - an energetic arrangement.'

'It has been used extensively by a number of great musicians worldwide.'

Rouben drove the car out of the underground parking lot onto the street and headed towards the Republic Square, where the colourful fountains were co-ordinated with lights and soft music in the evenings. The surrounding illuminated government buildings and museum gave the square a stately air.

'You can particularly enjoy Yerevan by night here,' Rouben said. 'A great place to just sit back on one of the benches and watch people as they pass by.'

'Also a great place to clear your mind, isn't it?' I asked with a smile.

'Absolutely,' he affirmed.

He drove along another back street and dropped me at the hotel.

'Thanks for the invitation,' I said.

'Don't mention it,' he replied with a smile.

# Chapter 23

I gathered from some local Armenians that the new adolescents of present-day Armenia had a better subconscious perception of independence and no longer believed in Soviet ideas. They acknowledged that many of the propagandized teachings of the former Soviet regime were false. Since Armenia had achieved independence, a new light had been shed on such old and fixed ideas, as a result of the youth's changing ideologies. These adolescents were throwing off the influence of Soviet cultural values and did not take an interest in Armenian politics for they had a deep mistrust of the current political system and this cast an air of pessimism over the future of Armenia. In fact, they did not believe the government wanted to improve the situation in the country because the political elite pursued the interests of their leaders, not of the ordinary people.

In large cities, Armenian youth who were knowledgeable about the modern world had embraced a more liberal Western culture – rock and popular music – and frequently visited discos, nightclubs, and internet clubs. Those who lived in rural areas on very low incomes were unable to share these privileges. Moreover, they were suffering from limited access to educational opportunities, diminishing their chances on the labour market. Some areas were even facing depopulation as a result of migration to urban areas or abroad. However, both urban and rural groups appeared to be moving nowadays toward a bi-cultural identity without abandoning their parents' traditions.

Armenian society tended to be a collective society with strong traditions, and a typical Armenian family maintained traditional values and took pride in discipline and strict moral standards. But globalization had been affecting Armenian urban youth in areas such as interdependence, attitudes toward marriage, and customs regarding courtship and marriage. Young Armenian families tended to be more independent and build their own nuclear families. The statistical age of marriage had also changed. In comparison with the past years, Armenians were not inclined to get married very young. They wanted to build their careers and achieve success first. They were more interested in studying languages belonging to the European continent.

Yerevan, at least in its outer appearance, could pass for any other European city, but behind the scenes living conditions were still bleak. The retired couple who spent their days at home were dreaming of a better life for their children. Most of the locals could not afford the luxuries in downtown. I reflected for a moment on how the slow pace of life in the city was vastly different from the stressful daily-grind reality of American life. It struck me that, for the average tourist, the cost of living in Armenia was incredibly low, and anyone with some capital - whether retired or not - could live a comfortable life.

Since Armenia moved from a presidential to parliamentary system, its human rights record had remained patchy, with serious concerns over media freedom, poor prison conditions, ill-treatment of children in boarding schools, and discrimination against women. A comprehensive anti-discrimination law, applying to all forms and grounds of discrimination, had not yet been adopted by the government of Armenia. During the election in June 2015, more than 5000 protesters took to the streets to denounce fuel price hikes and excessive police violence. Demonstrators lined the streets, ignoring a call to disperse and digging in for a new day of action. About 240 arrests, among them women, had been made in connection with the unrest. Police violated the right to freedom of assembly and detained many reporters, in some cases confiscating cameras and deleting photos/videos of the events.

According to Human Rights in Armenia (HRA), important legal safeguards for juveniles formulated by the legislators remained on paper. In the same year, eighty juveniles, some of them females, were tried before Armenian courts and in some cases sent to prison. In fact, Armenia lacked separate legislation on juvenile justice. There were no specialized juvenile courts or specially-appointed judges dealing only with such cases. The same gap existed in the prosecution system – no specialized unit for the investigation and criminal prosecution of juvenile cases. The lack of resources had always been a pretext for the government to avoid investment in this field.

On the other hand, there was wide-spread public opinion that Armenia's penitential system was mostly repressive and not conducive to re-socialization and re-integration of offenders back into society. This entailed the higher risk of re-offending and further alienation after release from prison. There were numerous reports published by commissioners who addressed important issues, such as the problems of the judicial system in Armenia, lack of effective investigation into allegations of torture and ill-treatment, overuse of pre-trial detention as a measure of restraint, and non-combat killings in the army.

# Chapter 24

My two-week trip was coming to an end. I couldn't believe I had only two days left. Time had flown by and it felt like only yesterday that I was stepping out of the plane into the Zvartnots airport. Rouben called me at the hotel and suggested taking me to "Vernissage"; an open-air market where tourists could buy souvenirs. I agreed and he picked me up from the hotel in the afternoon.

'This is a good place if you want to go shopping in Armenia,' he said. 'You can find so many interesting handcrafted items made by the locals; things you would never imagine.'

After five minutes' drive we reached the place, located between the Republic Square and Khanjian Street, close to many hotels. Rouben parked the car and we made our way into the huge market, which was crowded with tourists, artists, and curious individuals strolling around the place and chatting with stallholders. There was a vast range of second-hand stuff there like old watches, badges, coins, medallions, and Soviet-made videos and cameras. The market at first looked like a bazaar sale, similar to markets of Asian countries, but the deeper we went inside, the better the items we found – wooden crafts, musical instruments, swords and knives. Further ahead, silver and stone jewellery was displayed, along with bracelets, earrings, and necklaces. As a woman stopped to look, I noticed that the vendor was friendly but not pushy.

'Do sellers at the market speak English?' I asked Rouben.

He shook his head, 'Most of them do not, but they often know a few English phrases or else have a buddy to help.' He then whispered in my ear, 'When making purchases, if you let the seller know you're a tourist, the prices will go higher than they actually are.'

'Oh, really?' I asked, amazed.

'This is an annoying problem for locals, who are sometimes being taken for foreigners and asked the same price tourists would be required to pay.'

'Is bargaining acceptable here?' I asked.

'Of course, you can bargain for just about everything! But it is only occasionally successful; it all depends on who you're with and what you want.'

We walked past traditional waistcoats, weaves, trinkets, and a string of hand-embroidered handkerchiefs and tablecloths, some of them with letters of the Armenian alphabet in the form of birds. We then made our way into another part of the market, where numerous colourful Armenian rugs were on display with traditional patterns and ornaments.

'Are these handmade?' I asked.

'Not all of them,' Rouben said.

'A handmade carpet should be expensive.'

He nodded. 'The price usually starts from a few thousand dollars.'

We paused to take a look at the oil paintings produced by local amateur artists. Outdoor scenery of landscapes and Mount Ararat were the main themes of impressionist painters. There were also abstract paintings depicting flowers in a vase or fruits on a silver plate. We then walked up to a bazaar-like place dotted with stalls, where thousands of second-hand books – hardback and paperback – in Armenian, Russian and English were laid out in tidy piles on several long tables and on the floor. As we stopped there for a while, the owner; an old lady with wrinkles and grey hair, held her hand out in welcome. I looked at the English titles. The choice was extensive – classic literature, biographies and memoirs, some old bestsellers, cookery books, etc.

After about quarter of an hour, the lady asked, 'Can I be of any assistance?'

'Well, I'm looking for something in English about Armenian customs and traditions.'

She walked to the adjacent table, pulled one book out of the pile and handed it to me with a smile. After leafing through it, I asked the lady, 'How much?'

'1500 drams,' she said.

'Okay,' I agreed and paid her the amount.

As we walked away, Rouben asked, surprised, 'You've come all the way here to buy just an old book?'

'This will be a souvenir from the Armenian Vernissage,' I replied with a smile.

'You call that a souvenir?'

'There's not really anything else I want but I didn't want to leave empty-handed.'

'The ongoing socio-economic situation has considerably reduced the number of book-buyers in this country. Gone are the days when young people would read a famous piece of literature. There was a time when we prided ourselves on having the greatest number of readers.'

'The internet has also made a huge change in people's lives,' I said. 'You can read today online anything you like, no need to go to bookshops.'

'You're right,' he said.

We walked out of the market and back to his car. He turned onto Khanjian Street and after a short while pulled over to show me the Yerevan Chess House; a triangular-shaped three-storey building with sculpted images of chessmen on its curved façade. 'The chess house is named after the former world champion, Tigran Petrosian, known as Iron Tigran due to his safe playing style and strong defence. There's his statue there beside the building, can you see it?'

I nodded as he continued, 'The building serves as the home of both the Chess School and the Chess Federation of Armenia. We're a big player in world chess; it is a national obsession in this country. One needs to have the skill of seeing and tackling a threat ten to twenty moves before it materializes. Young children of six and seven are given obligatory chess lessons in our schools.'

'I'm sure kids today could learn to play the game faster than adults,' I said.

'Because they don't have as many responsibilities as adults do,' he agreed.

While Rouben drove me back to the hotel, he said, 'Another chess grand master and world champion was the Russian Gary Kasparov, of Armenian descent.'

Rouben asked me about my flight time the next day. I told him it was at 11.00 a.m. and that I would take a taxi but he insisted on taking me to the airport himself. So we arranged to meet in the hotel's lobby the next day, two hours before the flight was scheduled.

# Chapter 25

The next morning, Rouben called me from the hotel's lobby. I carried my luggage down to the reception desk and checked out of the hotel. With the luggage in the trunk of Rouben's car, we were on our way to the airport.

'Well, what are your first impressions of Armenia?' Rouben asked curiously.

'A fascinating country with a rich cultural heritage and a recorded history; also, incredible landscapes. I'm thrilled to have had the opportunity to go to a country I'd never thought I would be able to visit, and see so many monuments and churches in just two weeks.'

'Many of those locals haven't been yet to such fantastic places, you know. Our country is called "the museum under the open sky".'

'Absolutely,' I said. 'When visiting a place for the first time you can't help but to compare it to your home country and note the differences.'

'Everyone does the same. Can I ask you a personal question?'

'Of course,' I said.

'What do you think of Armenia as a homeland for all Armenians?'

'You can call any place where you belong "home". It depends on how every individual looks at it. Armenians conceptualize home in terms of lived experiences in their host countries. For instance, I personally feel much more like a tourist here than in Boston.'

Rouben nodded in agreement, 'Most of the diasporan Armenians feel that way and think they're tourists in their own country, but I suppose your tour experiences have helped strengthen your Armenian identity.'

'To a certain extent, yes,' I replied and added, 'I can certainly say now I'm part-Armenian and part-American.'

Rouben pulled over at the entrance to the airport. He took my luggage out of the trunk of his car and put it beside me.

'Thanks so much for everything,' I said.

'My pleasure,' he smiled.

Immediately after he finished speaking, I noticed tears welling in his eyes. He looked away in an attempt to fight them back.

I patted Rouben on the shoulder and said, 'Hey, I had a wonderful time on all our tours, thanks to you. I'll come back one day.'

He looked back at me and we hugged for a few seconds. Then I released my hold of him and picked up my luggage.

'Have a safe journey home!' he said.

'Thanks, and take care.'

After we parted, I headed to the airline desk and checked in. Having received my boarding pass, I went through security and found my gate. I stayed seated in the boarding area and it struck me that the brightly-lit departure lounge on the terminal's upper level was much more modern than its dimly-lit ground-floor hall for the arrivals. After a while, my zone was called and we started boarding the plane in an orderly fashion. I took my window seat and noticed there were not too many passengers on board the flight to Paris, where I had to catch a connecting flight to Boston. We fastened our seatbelts and just a few minutes later the plane took off.

As it began a steep climb to 27,000 feet, I looked back on the time I had spent in Armenia with Rouben, who really went out of his way and made every day a blast. His level of current and historical knowledge was impressive.

With time, our relationship had unexpectedly become more informal, as a certain closeness grew up between us. I fully remunerated him, for he was an excellent guide; enthusiastic and entertaining.

The local Armenians, young and old, were hospitable, curious and benevolent people. They took pride in ensuring their guests were treated well and some sort of gift was usually part of their hospitality. When I passed through some villages with Rouben, I was greeted warmly and invited for a coffee, then shared a meal with the residents, during which we talked about me and my trip to Armenia. It felt like spending the day visiting long-lost relatives and sharing my thoughts with them. Their faces remained in my memory.

Despite all the places I had visited, there were still moments where the feeling of not belonging was all-consuming. It happened randomly when I interacted with some locals in downtown. A casual conversation that I thought I would enjoy suddenly disappointed me. I was acutely aware of the fact that I didn't fit in that place with the people around me. I didn't know what specifically triggered that feeling for me. It could be just the realms of ideas or patterns of daily life, or something related to the economic difficulties, or to the Soviet legacy which was still present in Armenia. It was not surprising how many diaspora Armenians like me felt the same way right now.

The United States remained my own country, to which I had become accustomed, immersing myself in its culture. The long return flight from Paris to Boston left me enough time to reflect on my exploration of Armenia and plan how I would translate all my experiences into a series of articles for the paper over a month or two, with photos of historic sites. I would focus, among other things, on Armenia's turbulent past, challenging present, and homeland-diaspora relationship. I had already decided what angle I needed to take and how I would connect related content together to encourage readers to return for the next instalment. Finally, I would entitle my work *Gateway to Armenia*.

# Epilogue

In late January 2017, the first instalment appeared in the *Boston Daily* on its culture page, accompanied by a first photo of the Temple of Garni. My colleagues, who had never heard of this country, read the article with interest and asked me some questions about my trip. I said that I was lucky enough to have an excellent private guide for my tours, during which I tried to capture a purely objective record of what I explored and experienced in Armenia. My aim was to take an investigative look at each site in order to bring greater meaning to places and provide important insights into Armenia's history through my explorations and own researches.

Asked about the challenges facing present-day Armenia, I said that they are daunting; there are the economic and political challenges, and significant internal problems, such as the mounting social divide between a wealthy elite and an impoverished segment of the population. The country's biggest problem was the rampant corruption at all levels. One external challenge is the blockade of Armenia by Turkey and Azerbaijan, preventing natural trade and economic development. About the local people, I said I always kept an open mind to learn about their lives, customs and traditions.

On the same day, I received congratulatory emails from the staff of Armenian newspapers. They said that they would look forward to reading the upcoming articles on Armenia. Within the next month, the remaining three instalments - one each week - appeared in the paper, with various photos of historical monuments and museums. I received many reviews of my work from Armenian and non-Armenian readers alike, and I thanked them all.

The following year, in early May 2018, mass street protests in Armenia – seen as a 'velvet revolution' that began with only a couple of dozen people a month earlier – eventually forced the resignation of the country's Prime Minister and the government. This unexpected event won the praise of the diaspora Armenian communities and the world. It was the beginning of the creation of a new democratic Armenia based on justice.